the
SECRET LANGUAGE
of Cats

the
SECRET LANGUAGE
of Cats

THE BODY LANGUAGE OF FELINE BODIES

Heather Dunphy

METRO BOOKS
New York

METRO BOOKS
New York

An Imprint of Sterling Publishing
387 Park Avenue South
New York, NY 10016

Conceived, designed, and produced by
Quid Publishing
Level 4 Sheridan House
114 Western Road
Hove BN3 1DD
England
www.quidpublishing.com

Design: Ali Walper

ISBN 978-1-4351-3778-3

For information about custom editions, special sales, and premium and corporate purchases,
please contact Sterling Special Sales at 800-805-5489 or specialsales@sterlingpublishing.com.

Manufactured in China

5 7 9 10 8 6 4

www.sterlingpublishing.com

CONTENTS

INTRODUCTION

*T*he ancestry of the domestic cat and the story of how its relationship with humans has evolved plots a fascinating journey through history. The cat was revered, persecuted, and gradually made its way from working our barns to entering our homes and hearts. But why and how were cats first domesticated? Typically, wild animals were domesticated for what they could provide: milk, meat, wool, or labor. Cats don't provide us with food, nor do they herd other animals, pull sleds, or act as security; they are, however, experts at catching small prey. Most experts agree that domestication occurred when cats started hunting the rodents that fed on grain stores, which resulted in wild cats living in closer proximity to human settlements. This brought them to the notice of people and began their journey of domestication, a long and often difficult road for our felines.

FROM WILD CAT TO DOMESTIC CAT

The earliest archaeological evidence of the domestication of cats is a very recent find. In 2004, Jean-Denis Vigne of the National Museum of Natural History in Paris unearthed two graves on the island of Cyprus with the help of his colleagues. These graves contained the remains of a human and a cat that date back over 9,500 years. Since cats are not native to most Mediterranean islands, experts agree that this find indicates an intentional relationship between human and feline. This predates what we know of the cat in ancient Egypt, where it was long believed that domestication took place. We do know that ancient Egyptians worshipped cats and believed them to be in close contact with deities and gods. Thought to ward off evil spirits, the cat was mummified when dead and protected in life by the laws of the time. He was valued for his prowess as a hunter and celebrated in art, as seen in sculpture and tomb paintings of the ancient Egyptian empire. Paintings from Egypt's golden era, approximately 3,600 years ago, show unmistakable signs of feline domestication, with cats pictured wearing collars or eating from bowls. Though a strict ban on the export of cats was in place, they were nonetheless smuggled out of Egypt and onto the ships of traders, with their hunting skills effectively acting as a passport around the globe. They were brought on long voyages to keep rats and mice at bay and soon found themselves at home in new lands.

All this is evidence of the long-standing relationship between cats and people, but the question of domestication remains: did people domesticate cats, or did cats domesticate themselves? It seems likely, as adherents to the latter theory believe, that the solitary wild cats—unlike other animals who were removed from the wild by humans—made the choice to go where the hunting was good, and that meant adapting to human settlements. Cats moved closer to people to be near the granaries that were fertile hunting grounds. People recognized the value of these cats, who were not interested in their grain but more concerned with hunting the rodents stealing it, and encouraged the feline presence. A win-win situation for both.

⊛ Cat Fact

There are approximately ten million pet cats in Britain, and about 93 million pet cats in the United States.

DOMESTICATION TIMELINE

Although the exact timeline of cat domestication remains uncertain, approximate dates are generally agreed upon.

- 8000 BC: Archaeological evidence of the domestication of cats is found in a grave on the island of Cyprus.
- 3500 BC: Domestication of the African wild cat in Egypt.
- 900 BC: Cats imported from Egypt arrive in Italy.
- 500 BC: Domestic cat is established in China.
- 300 BC: Phoenician traders bring cats to India.
- 100 BC: Cats fall out of favor in Egypt as they become increasingly widespread.
- AD 600: Buddhist monks introduce the cat to Japan.
- AD 1620: Cats are introduced to North America, traveling there with pilgrims on the *Mayflower* and other ships.
- AD 1749: Colonists of the New World send for cats from Europe to counter the problems brought by infestation of rats.
- AD 1758: Method of zoological classification is established and the domestic cat is given the binomial name *Felis catus*.
- AD 1866: The American Society for the Prevention of Cruelty to Animals (ASPCA) is formed, based on the Royal Society for the Prevention of Cruelty to Animals (RSPCA) in London.
- AD 1871: The first cat show is held at Crystal Palace in London.
- AD 1872: *The Expressions of Emotions in Man and Animals* by Charles Darwin is published, in which he examines feline emotions and body language.
- AD 1895: First American cat show held at Madison Square Garden in New York.
- AD 1900s: Scientist Louis Pasteur discovers microbe that reveals the hygienic habits of the cat.
- AD 1910: The Governing Council of the Cat Fancy (GCCF) is formed.
- AD 1946: Spaying of cats is encouraged through the charity, Cats Protection.
- AD 1953: The Governing Council of the Cat Fancy holds its first cat show.

FROM HUNTER TO HUNTED

In the Middle Ages in Europe, the tide turned against cats. Thanks to their aloofness, independence, and nocturnal lifestyle, cats came to be thought of as pagan. The church led an inquisition against them and they were slaughtered en masse, which led to their near-extinction in 1400. When the bubonic plague arrived in Europe in the fourteenth century, there weren't enough cats remaining to help contain the rat population. This contributed to the disease spreading rapidly through medieval Europe, killing approximately 25 million people—one-third of the European population.

By the 1800s, feline fortunes had improved. Laws were passed forbidding animal mistreatment and felines were once more a favored pet. Their popularity continued to increase and by the mid-nineteenth century they were being selectively bred for specific traits, such as their color, coat, and personality. The popularity of the domestic cat also increased thanks to its fastidious cleaning habits, which gave it a reputation as a hygienic pet. With breeding came national and international cat shows and cat fancy organizations, which brings us to the present. Today the cat is a commonplace fixture in our homes, with more than 600 million cats living among humans worldwide.

SECRET LANGUAGE

Regardless of their breed or appearance, cats continue to share a common trait inherited from their ancestors—that of the solitary hunter. They are designed to hunt, and this trait, which initially made them so valued by humans, remains evident today—regardless of whether they are farm cats that patrol the barn for mice or urban apartment-dwelling cats that play at hunting in the living room. All cats also share a common cat language, with a vocabulary of body language, scent, and vocalization. A slowly swishing tail accompanied by a focused and intense gaze is one many cat owners will be familiar with. It signals that the cat is getting ready to pounce and it is a predatory behavior. It is just one of the many messages cats communicate through body language, and when we learn to read the signs we understand the secret language of our felines. There are the more obvious signals such as the arched spine, which signals fear or aggression; there are also the less obvious, such as the head bunting movement cats will practice with their humans. The latter combines body language with scent communication—a very important communication tool for cats given their highly developed sense of smell—to leave a territorial message. By bunting heads, the cat deposits some of his scent onto you. This is a clear message to other felines and a

Cute Cats

Although empirical research into the theory is not exactly abundant, it has been speculated that the physiological proportions of the cat's face may have played a part in their evolutionary success. It is thought by some that the large eyes and snub face of the wild cat may have contributed to our ease in bonding with them, as those features are known to invoke nurturing instincts in humans. These facial features are evident in breeds such as the Birman, Shorthair Exotic, and Persian Longhair.

reassuring reminder to your cat that you are part of what he considers his. Our cats also communicate through scent marking. They claw at objects to leave visible marks and to release pheromones from the scent glands in their paws, just as their relative in the wild, the lion, does. That scent message may be accompanied by vocalization as well, such as the enigmatic meow. This familiar sound can mean different things depending on its pitch, volume, and the context in which it is uttered, so its translation is best made by paying attention not only to the sound but to your cat's accompanying actions. This is true for the other vocalizations your cat may use as well, such as the purr, chatter, and hiss.

We attribute human responses and motivation to our cats, and this assumption that our feline acts as we

🐾 Cat Fact

Before our cave-dwelling ancestors discovered words, we communicated using body language and the occasional sound, just as our felines do.

do contributes to misunderstandings. It is important to remember that cats are not four-legged humans who feel and react to things as we do. One example: the cat who plays with live prey before killing it. Speak to any cat-lover who has witnessed this—there will be many—and they are generally horrified. That act, they say, doesn't seem like something their cat would do. It seems too cruel, and very unlike their feline. When we set out to learn the secret language of our cats it is important to remember that there are three sides to every story: yours, the cat's, and the truth.

In this example, the cat's actions seem a cruel act if we look at it only through our own eyes. Through the eyes of a cat, however, playing with prey has a different significance, and contrary to what we might like to believe, it is a very feline act. Our cats don't dangle the mouse and move it forward and back for amusement, but because the mouse may bite, so they are tiring it out. Our cats are predators and it was this trait that made domestication desirable, just as it is this trait that brought your cat's ancestors to the area you call home so many years ago. If we remember this, it gives us insight into our feline. They don't see playing with prey as cruel; it's just practical and a part of who they are.

Cats have left their paw prints on art, religion, and politics. They are a different species, but one with a history intertwined with ours. They communicate through a different language, but by looking at what makes a cat a cat, it is a language that we can learn. Their history provides insight into our own history and our bond with our felines ensures there is much more to come from our continued relationship.

Communication with Our Cats

Familiarity with how a cat uses body language and vocalization to communicate is the first step in learning feline language. To translate fully, it is helpful to look at how facial expressions, ear set, tail carriage, body language, posture, and sound come together to express emotion or intention. They are the vocabulary of feline language and when combined they form a distinct message. In any other combination the vocabulary may mean something else, just as the way we string words together in English forms sentences that have different meanings.

No. 1 FIRST IMPRESSIONS

PEDIGREE AND DOMESTIC CATS

"There are no ordinary cats."
—Colette, author

*B*ritain has approximately ten million pet cats in a population of about 61 million people. In the United States, there are approximately 93.6 million pet cats, with 33 percent of U.S. households owning at least one cat. The number of cat registries, breed societies, and cat clubs worldwide demonstrate how widespread cat ownership is throughout the world, a fact understandable to those lucky enough to already share their life with a cat.

🐾 Cat Fact

Knowing the secret language of purebred and mixed-breed cat characteristics helps you to better understand your cat.

If you have decided to join the growing numbers of cat owners, you first need to decide what kind of cat is most suited to you. Most cats don't come with papers, but, if you have your heart set on one that does, then it's helpful to know about the recognized breeds so that you can choose the pedigreed cat that best matches your lifestyle. Do you want a comforting lap cat, or an energetic entertainer? A cat with a long luxurious coat, or one that will need less grooming? Does an independent cat suit your busy schedule, or do you want one that enjoys interaction and will be a companion for you throughout the day? Every cat is special and unique but breeds do share characteristics that can help you determine your best feline match. Depending on their breed they can be aloof or social, relaxed or active, mischievous or inquisitive. Understanding the different breed characteristics is a small investment in time, but well worth it since your cat may be part of your life for 15 or more wonderful years.

BEHIND THE SIGNS

Kitten or Cat?

If you bring a cat into your home, it is important first to consider how their age may help or hinder their integration into the family. A new kitten requires a lot of time for grooming, socialization, training, and play. An older cat is typically already socialized and their exercise needs are less demanding than a kitten's. Whichever you decide, know that both are able to bond equally well and that age is no deterrent to forming a close relationship.

☙ Cat Fact

There are new cat breeds recognized yearly, despite the stringent rules. Newly recognized breeds are classified as spontaneous mutations (like the Scottish Fold, for example) or are created by the purposeful hybridization of two or more breeds.

Breeds are recognized differently throughout the world, according to the cat registries or breed societies of that country. Some countries have one cat fancy organization that focuses on appreciation, promotion, and breeding of cats, while in others, such as the United States, there are multiple organizations. The number of breeds recognized also varies; the Governing Council of the Cat Fancy (GCCF) in Britain, for example, recognizes approximately 100 breeds, while the US-based Cat Fancier's Association (CFA)—the largest cat fancy organization in the world—recognizes approximately 40 breeds.

Catwalk Competition

Although cat shows focus on purebred cats, many cat associations also have a Household Pet Category (HPC) in which mixed-breed and domestic cats can compete. If you are interested in showing your cat, you can find entry rules and cat show dates through your local or national cat fancy organizations. Cat associations rarely limit their work to organizing cat shows; they often set breed standards, provide numerous training opportunities, including for show judges, and also inspect catteries to ensure national and international standards of care are maintained to a high level.

CAT REGISTRIES AND CLUBS

Here are a selection from around the world that can provide further information on cat breeds as well as opportunities to get involved in showing your pedigreed or domestic cat.

AUSTRALIA
• Australian Cat Federation, Inc. (ACF) www.acf.asn.au

• Waratah National Cat Alliance (WNCA)www.wnca.com.au

BRITAIN
• Governing Council of the Cat Fancy (GCCF) www.gccfcats.org

CANADA
• Canadian Cat Association/ Association Féline Canadienne (CCA/AFC) www.cca-afc.com

INTERNATIONAL
• Cat Fancier's Association (CFA) www.cfainc.org

• International Cat Association (TICA) www.tica.org

• Traditional Cat Association (TCA) www.traditionalcats.com

• World Cat Federation www.wcf-online.de

NEW ZEALAND
• New Zealand Cat Fancy (NZCF) www.nzcatfancy.gen.nz

SOUTH AFRICA
• Cat Federation of Southern Africa (CFSA) www.cfsa.co.za

• Southern Africa Cat Council (SACC) www.tsacc.org.za

UNITED STATES
• American Association of Cat Enthusiasts, Inc. (AACE) www.aaceinc.org

• American Cat Fancier's Association (ACFA) www.acfacat.com

PEDIGREED CATS

Abyssinian: Elegant and sleekly muscular in appearance, with yellow-green eyes and a medium-length and distinct agouti-marked (ticked or flecked) coat that gives them a jungle look. They are known to be high-spirited, clownish, entertaining, loyal, and people-oriented, although they do not usually like to be held and are not lap-sitters. They don't shed much and need only a weekly brushing. The Abyssinian is one of the oldest cat breeds, with depictions of this breed found in ancient Egyptian artwork.

American Shorthair: These cats are strongly built and of medium size with middle-of-the-road temperament. They like being with you but don't force themselves on you, and they are active but not hyper. American Shorthairs are friendly, playful cats who want to be part of their owners' life but are not needy. They are great family cats and good for first-time owners, and they get along well with other cats and pets. Their short coat doesn't mat and is self-cleaning, so they require almost no grooming. Interestingly, it is believed that these cats—descended from the British Shorthair—came to the US with pilgrims on the *Mayflower*, who valued them for their superior mousing ability.

Bengal: Very gregarious, lively, and curious, this dedicated hunter is often on the move. These cats have a stunning shorthaired coat that is spotted and was inherited from the leopard from which they were bred. Bengals are attracted to water, whether that means a swim, or playing with the running water from a tap.

Birman: Loyal companions who enjoy spending time with people. Some would say they are more dog-like than cat-like, although, like their feline counterparts, they too enjoy being adored—something that is perhaps even more ingrained in the Birman, given the legend that they were bred as temple cats. Their medium- to longhaired coat does not mat but does need regular grooming.

Cornish Rex: High-energy and extroverted cats who love to jump and climb. They are very curious and

love games, but are also people-oriented and enjoy lap sitting. These cats have a distinctive short coat that is tight and curly and sheds little. They need minimal brushing but need frequent bathing to keep clean.

Devon Rex: Very affectionate, loyal, playful, and fearless cats, easily recognized by their wavy coat and very large ears and eyes that give them an otherworldly appearance. These cats like to stay close, perching on or near you, and they love to cuddle.

They typically need frequent bathing due to their coat type, but shed less than most breeds and need minimal brushing.

BEHIND THE SIGNS

Cat Confusion

Their names are similar, they look similar but, as breeders are quick to point out, there are big differences between the American Shorthair and the Domestic Shorthaired (often known as the American Domestic in the US). The latter is not a breed but is a name given to all mixed-breed cats by cat fancy organizations. Because the Domestic Shorthaired are of mixed ancestry, their temperament and appearance are not true to any one breed, as it is with the American Shorthairs, who are pedigreed cats with known ancestry.

Exotic (also known as Exotic Shorthair):
Similar to the Persian in temperament and looks but with a shorthaired coat that is very plush, giving them a soft, rounded appearance.  Their coats don't mat but they do shed and will need weekly brushing. They are good lap cats: quiet, mellow, and affectionate companions. They love attention but are not overly demanding, although they like to stay close. With their easy-going and adaptable temperament, the Exotic is a good feline match for families.

Maine Coon: A native American longhaired cat, first developed as a breed in Maine. Valued for their hunting skills, their likeable personalities soon made them one of the most popular breeds in the US. They have a hardy disposition, are intelligent, lovable, and affectionate, although they can be aloof with strangers. Their coat is silky and thick, their paws are oversized (for better navigation in the snow), and they have an identifiable "M" on their foreheads. Because of their sweet temperament and adult size—approximately 15–25 pounds—they are known as "gentle giants."

Munchkin: Affectionate, intelligent, and playful cats, equally happy during a game of chase or when on their owner's lap. They can have short- or longhaired coats and are distinctive due to their short and stubby legs, reminiscent of the dachshund dog. Munchkins have caused controversy amongst cat fanciers, with some finding their short legs a problem.

Oriental: Similar in looks and behavior to a Siamese. They love nothing more than spending time with you and they will make sure you know it. They can be very vocal and they need attention. In return they are loyal, affectionate, and playful, as well as curious and intelligent family members. These elegant-looking cats are athletic and can be short- or longhaired. They are easy to groom: the shorthaired coat is self-cleaning and needs only the occasional brushing to add shine, while the longhaired Oriental requires weekly brushing.

Persian (also known as Persian Longhair):

One of the oldest and most popular of cat breeds, Persians tend to be gentle and placid. They like routine and do well in peaceful surroundings, but are generally adaptable to more lively environments as long as they are made to feel secure. They are regal in bearing, as befitting a favorite cat of the aristocracy, but are also playful, affectionate, and loyal. They enjoy attention but are typically not demanding. They have a low activity level, in part due to their short legs and a stocky, compact body type known as "cobby," which contributes to slower movement and less jumping and climbing agility. Their long flowing coat means their body temperature can increase sharply with exercise and their flattened face—a shape known as brachycephalic—affects breathing, making respiration more difficult for the Persian when exercising than is the case with fuller-faced breeds. These cats live to lounge and coexist peacefully with other cats, dogs, and children. They have large eyes that tear easily, so a daily face wash is recommended, as well as daily brushing to avoid mats and hairballs.

Ragdoll: Their name suits these cats well as they may relax completely and go limp in a person's arms. They are sweet-tempered and adaptable to different environments, and are playful but laid-back. They are often described as puppy-like because of the manner in which they follow their owners from room to room. They have very bright blue oval-shaped eyes and their coat is semi-long and very soft, with minimal grooming necessary. These are cuddly, big-boned cats that grow to a very large size and can be three times larger than most other felines.

🐾 Cat Fact

Mixed breeds have been with us for thousands of years and are a diverse grouping of felines of different temperaments, coat colors, and patterns. They are not recognized as a breed because of their mixed ancestry; however, many of the purebred cats we know today owe their start to them.

Siamese: An ancient cat breed, originally from Siam (now known as Thailand) where they were bred as aristocratic cats. These cats are intelligent, curious, athletic, and affectionate. They have a social temperament and may sometimes gravitate to one family member in particular. They like to be with their people and are known chatterers, "talking" in their characteristic yowl. These cats are partially albino and are born white, with color developing on their head, feet, and tail. They have a striking appearance, with their coat of contrasting colors, blue almond-shaped eyes, and long, sleek appearance. They are easy to groom and good family pets, but their very vocal chattering and purring can be enjoyable or annoying depending on your perspective.

Russian Blue: These cats are playful and affectionate with their chosen people, but typically shy and aloof or absent with strangers. They are active yet gentle and quiet cats who like routine and cleanliness. They enjoy time spent with their family but are also good at entertaining themselves. Their expression is as sweet-tempered as their personality, with the slight upturn of their mouth giving the appearance of a constant smile. Their unique double coat is short, plush, and dense—and is often compared to the coat of a seal in texture—and is a gray-blue color with a silver sheen.

Sphynx: Easily recognizable because of their lack of coat, this breed is unique and exotic-looking, as well as being very mischievous, active—they particularly love to climb—family-oriented and loyal. These cats demand attention and are very loving and affectionate in return.

Laid-Back or High-Energy?

Different activity levels between cat breeds are often a result of size and shape. Fuller-figured and heavier-coated breeds, such as the Persian, are more lethargic and less playful than sleeker shorthaired breeds like the lively Siamese, or the svelte and hairless Sphynx. If you want your cat to be a more active member of the family who will happily play and engage in physical activity, you may want to steer clear of the longhaired breeds.

DOMESTIC CATS

Most cat-owners are the proud and happy owners of domestic cats. In many places in the world, these cats account for 90 percent of the feline pet population. This number is influenced by price, as mixed-breed cats are typically inexpensive; availability, as shelters and humane societies are overflowing; but also because these cats are just as lovable as pedigreed cats. Cat fancy organizations call these mixed-breed cats either domestic shorthaired or domestic longhaired. They are also known as "moggies" and are sometimes referred to as tabby cats. The latter name is not exclusive to mixed-breed cats, however, as is sometimes thought, and it is not a breed name. Instead, it refers to a coat pattern—striped, spotted, swirled, patched—that can be found in many pedigreed and mixed-breed cats. Domestic cats have varied facial expressions and body shapes, depending on where in the world they were born and from what gene pool. As a result, there is no breed standard to use as a guide as to what they may look like as they develop. They may be petite or large, longhaired or shorthaired, and there is a wide assortment of coat colors and patterns they may inherit.

Since they are from mixed ancestry, domestic cats' temperaments can be just as unknown and varied as their adult appearance. They can be relaxed or active, shy or gregarious, inquisitive, mischievous, aloof, or affectionate, and any combination of these.

Pedigreed cats share characteristics of their breed, so their temperaments are more predictable. However, environment also plays a big role in determining the feline personality and likes and dislikes, for both pedigreed and mixed-breed cats. The most important factor in raising a happy and contented cat is to remember that all cats—regardless of ancestry—need our help to become the wonderful companions they are capable of being.

⊛ Cat Fact

Cats with a tortoiseshell or calico coat are almost always female.

YOUR BEST CAT MATCH

Which cat is right for you? Consider the amount of grooming needed. Some longhaired breeds need a minimum of a half-hour of grooming per day, while many shorthaired breeds need only twice-weekly brushing. This is not just to keep them looking good, but for health reasons as well. Matted hair attracts parasites; it can pull at tender skin, leaving it irritated, and it can lead to infections. Consider the amount of shedding as well. Longhaired breeds have more hair to shed, but all cats will shed a certain amount. That hair will be on your clothing and furniture; how much can you live with and how often will you be able to vacuum and dust? Are you or a family member allergic to cats? If so, consider one of the breeds that tend to elicit less reaction from allergy sufferers, such as the Cornish Rex. Do you want a lap cat? Then you may want to avoid some of the longhaired breeds, who get overly warm on laps and prefer to sit elsewhere. Do you want a cat that follows you from room to room, like the Oriental or the Sphynx, or do you want one that is less needy of attention, like the Russian Blue? Some breeds, like the Bengal, are high-energy, while Persians are more lethargic—which best suits your family and lifestyle? If you have children then you'll want a cat that gets along with them; one that is relaxed, adaptable, and social. It's easy to fall in love with a cat's appearance, but love at

Cat Fact

Cats represent a commitment of up to 15 years, possibly more. Although recognized as easier pets to care for than dogs, they too need attention and mental and physical stimulation—a job that should not be underestimated.

first sight doesn't always translate to the cat meeting your needs or you meeting his. If you are looking for a gregarious cat who will entertain you with his antics then the more reserved breeds may not be your best match. Some cats need more attention than you may have time for, while others need quiet time alone and are not a good match for a family seeking a social and involved companion.

Cat Allergies

Cat hair doesn't cause allergies, but the proteins in a cat's saliva and the sebaceous glands of the skin does, which can lead to nasal congestion, coughing, wheezing, and watery eyes. There are no hypoallergenic cats, but some allergy sufferers find that the Russian Blue, Siberian, Oriental Shorthair, Cornish Rex, Devon Rex, and the Sphynx, among others, cause less reaction than other breeds.

WELCOME HOME

UNDERSTAND EACH OTHER
FROM DAY ONE

"Watch a cat when it enters a room for the first time. It searches and smells about, it is not quiet for a moment, it trusts nothing until it has examined and made acquaintance with everything."
—Jean-Jacques Rousseau, philosopher

Cats are creatures of comfort first and foremost. Provide for their physical and emotional comfort and you earn the trust needed to have the closest relationship possible. From the first day, work to give your relationship the right start by helping your cat easily adapt to your home so that you can then make a smooth transition to speaking each other's language.

You can change a first impression, but it takes a lot more work to do so than getting things right from the start, especially when—in the case of cats—a good first impression is so easy to manage. It just takes a little planning and an understanding of what your cat will need to settle in safely and happily.

CAT PROOFING

We have all heard the saying that "curiosity killed the cat" and, while a bit drastic, it does highlight two very important truths: 1) cats are inquisitive by nature; 2) their natural curiosity can prove a danger to them. Look at your home through your cat's eyes and from your cat's height, keeping in mind that cats are expert jumpers and climbers. Remove anything that could prove a danger. This includes any houseplants, as there are many that can make your cat sick when eaten, such as the calla lily, chrysanthemum, daffodil, ivy, and lily—known to be extremely toxic to cats—mistletoe, philodendron, poinsettia, and more. Yarn has long been associated as a favorite plaything of cats, but it doesn't like them as much as they like it. Yarn can be a choking hazard or, if swallowed, can cause intestinal blockages, so it should be kept out of reach, along with needles, thread, buttons, and any other small and easy-to-swallow objects. Electrical cords are attractive to cats but when chewed present a very real danger,

so tuck them under carpets and behind furniture where your cat can't get at them. If that is not possible, encase them in plastic conduit to make access more difficult. Drapery cords are irresistible to cats, but our felines can get tangled up in pull cord loops and injure themselves in their panic to get free or pull on the cords in play and cause the drapes to come crashing down. Tie cords high enough up that even a jumping cat can't get at them. Appliance cords are just as tempting, and playing cat and mouse with cords that hang to the ground from a wall-mounted television or an ironing board, for example, can cause the appliance to come crashing down when the cord is "caught." Keep cords that are in permanent use, like those of home media equipment, flush to the wall and protected by plastic or blocked by furniture. Wrap cords of appliances used less frequently, like that of an iron, when not in use and keep them out of reach from an inquisitive cat's paws or teeth.

Keep all cleaning products in a locked cupboard, as most cats quickly figure out how to work latches, along with antifreeze or any other substances that could prove toxic. Check that all windows have tight-fitting and thick screens that your cat's claws or teeth can't tear, and that are sturdy enough to withstand your cat's weight if he pushes against it. Garbage bins—in the bathroom and

The sooner your cat adjusts to his new environment, the sooner he is ready to get to know you and let you get to know him. To help the transition go smoothly you will need a few supplies, including: a litter box, litter, and litter shovel; food and water bowls; a cozy cat basket or bed; a scratching post, and a few noise-making chew toys. A carrier is useful when you are bringing your cat home from the vet or the shelter, and it may become a cave-like resting place when your cat is home. Place a blanket or a few towels on the floor of the carrier to make it cozy for your cat, and leave the carrier door open so he can come and go.

Cat Fact

If you would put an item out of a baby's reach then it should definitely be out of the more mobile and scent-curious cat's reach.

kitchen—should have tight-fitting lids to keep cats away from choking hazards like disposable razors or bones. Toilet lids should always be kept down to prevent cats from falling in, especially small or feeble cats that could have difficulty climbing out. Keep washing machine and drier doors closed and—just in case—always check the machine's drums before starting them to be sure your cat has not curled up inside for a nap. Plastic bags can be magnets for cats so they should always be put immediately out of reach, no matter how cute your cat may look when playing with them. What can start out as fun can quickly turn to tragedy, as has been proven countless times, unfortunately. It is not uncommon for cats to get stuck in the handle of the bag and injure themselves in their panic to get free, or suffocate when getting trapped in the bag. Many cats love nothing more than jumping up onto the high shelf of your bookcases, so move anything breakable and check that there are no unstable shelves, and that jumpable structures are strong enough not to topple when landed on.

Cat proofing can take a bit of time, but once done it can keep your cat safe and also save you a lot of unnecessary breakage and destruction.

BEHIND THE SIGNS

Avoid a Big Welcome

Keep the environment tranquil for your cat's first few days. He should meet family members and other pets gradually, rather than all together, once he has started to feel at home. The message you want to send your cat is that he is in a safe and secure environment and he will only understand that and respond to it if he is given the time he needs to adjust. Crowding him with too many unfamiliar things will only extend the period needed to become accustomed to the new surroundings.

BEHIND THE SIGNS

First Impressions

Helping your cat to make a smooth transition is just one of the building blocks that establish a good relationship. Your cat will meet you halfway, but you must earn his trust and loyalty first. Remember that you have a long time ahead of you, so be patient; don't expect immediate results and avoid becoming impatient with him. Needless to say, any impatience on your part will be evident to your cat and may damage the trust that is crucial to a positive and happy relationship between the two of you.

HOME SWEET HOME

Now that you've cat-proofed your home, the next step is to designate one room as your cat's base for his first week with you, so he has time to adjust slowly without being overwhelmed. Have everything you need in that room: water and food bowls, a litter box, a cozy cat bed, a scratching post, and two or three cat toys. If possible, the room you choose should be the room where your cat's litter box will remain. This helps to avoid any house-training accidents and confusion at a later date, as some cats get temporarily confused when the litter box location is changed. Place the litter in a private corner, away from doors (or other sources of commotion in the room), and at a distance from the food bowl. If you are bringing a kitten home, you may want to place the litter box slightly closer so that they see it often and are reminded of where it is so that it is close enough for them to get to quickly. It should still be at least six feet away from their food bowl. Cats are private and fastidious—they don't like to use a litter box that doesn't offer a semblance of privacy, or is too close to the food they eat.

Arrange to bring your cat home on a day when you can be home all day, and in the morning if possible so your cat has a full day to settle in and get used to you before you have to leave him for the night. Use a cat carrier to bring him home and set it down in the designated room. Close the door to the room and then open the door of the carrier, but don't be surprised if your cat chooses to stay where he is.

This is a natural reaction, for both shy and social cats. Don't rush him; it's a new environment and he needs time to take it in. Instead, stay in the room and go about your business, occasionally offering him a treat to tempt him out. When he does leave the carrier, let him explore at will and don't make any attempt just yet to pick him up or set him on your lap. He needs to feel secure first before he can bond with you.

Leave cat toys out for him to play with and, once he starts to play, gently join in, backing off if he is not yet at ease. Some cats are settled within a couple of days, while others may take up to a month. Encourage lots of playtime, especially a play session before you go to sleep to tire your cat out. Given the choice, most cats would sleep all day and play most of the night, so begin the process of getting him on your schedule from the start.

After a day or two, once your cat is at ease in the one room, you can slowly introduce him to the rest of the house. Make sure it is a quiet time of the day and let him explore. Cats love to nap, so have sleeping areas for your cat placed around your house. Make sure that one or two are in sunny spots, as catnaps in the sun are a cat specialty. Start off right by cleaning the litter daily and ensuring your cat's water bowl is filled with fresh water whenever it's empty. When your cat's physical needs

Cat Fact

You will know your cat is at ease when he is no longer hiding, is eating, and is using his litter box.

BEHIND THE SIGNS

A Little Dignity, Please

Cats don't like to be constrained in general, and this translates to some felines not enjoying being picked up. It is necessary at times, however, and there is a preferred method: put one hand on your cat's chest behind his front legs, and use your other hand to scoop up his back end and rear legs. Even the most playful and clownish of cats take themselves seriously and this method has been proven to get a better reaction than that given when the cat is scooped up under one arm.

are taken care of he will be at ease and you can then start getting to know him, and understand better his behavior, body language, and occasional vocalizations.

NEW CAT, MEET RESIDENT PET

In multi-pet households, cats and dogs can get along just fine, as long as they are given the time they need to feel comfortable with each other. Keep them apart for the first day or two to avoid overwhelming your new cat with too much at once. Then start off gently, with scent association to get them used to each other before allowing a face-to-face meeting:

Cat to cat: Use one clean towel per cat and rub the cat's face gently with it. Place the towel that was used on the resident cat's face under the new cat's food dish, and vice versa.

Dog to cat: Use one clean towel, and gently rub the underside of the dog's paws with it a few times. Take a second towel and rub the cat's face with it. Place the towel that was used on the dog under the cat's food dish and vice versa.

Scent glands are located in the feline face and in the canine paws, so through the towels they get to know each

other gradually—very important when they will be sharing a home together. Smell is the most important sense for felines and canines and one of their main communication methods. After doing this daily for a few days, you can open the door that divides the animals slightly, letting them get a look at each other, but still keeping them apart. If introducing a dog, make sure he is on leash. A certain amount of hissing or growling may take place and this is normal; just don't let it go on for too long. After a few minutes, close the door, give them each their space, and then try again, rewarding them each with praise for any non-aggressive curiosity. Once they are used to seeing each other you are ready to have them meet in the same room. Even then, if a dog is involved, keep him on leash. Supervise your pets until you are sure they are consistently friendly with each other. As they get to know one another, you can move their individual food bowls closer together day by day so that, as in the towel exercise, they associate each other's presence with good things, like food. The amount of time this process takes varies in each situation: some pets may already be used to living with other animals, or have had lots of socialization with dogs or other cats, and so are better able to adjust quickly; some will need more time, from a few weeks to a few months, until they are coexisting quite happily.

LITTER BOX LEARNING

It's often said that cats don't need training to use a litter box, they just know. This may be true of some cats, but many need to be guided. Shovel the litter in front of your cat to give him the right idea if he seems unsure, but be prepared for house-training accidents, especially during tho first week. Your cat will be nervous, excited, and probably overstimulated because so much is new to him, which contributes to accidents in your home. Ignore these and encourage use of the litter box by putting it in a low-traffic corner, changing the litter daily, and using the shovel if necessary to demonstrate to your cat appropriate litter-box etiquette.

Consistency Is Key

Everyone in your home must understand the house rules and consistently communicate them to your cat. He may ignore these rules, as cats do, but if you ignore him when he misbehaves and reward him with attention when he behaves as you want him to (like jumping up onto his scratching post, instead of onto the kitchen table), he will eventually understand. Cats may be independent and some may be aloof, but they appreciate rewards and attention and will repeat behavior that provides them with positive reinforcement.

CATS AND CHILDREN

There are many cats that are social, adaptable, and relaxed, which make them good matches for households with children, as long as the children understand how to handle and play with a cat. This doesn't usually come naturally, so children should be taught in advance that cats respond well to gentle attention. They don't like to be chased, teased, or constrained. They should never be disturbed when eating or sleeping. Quick movements, loud noises, and rough play can be frightening for cats, especially when they are adjusting to the children, and the time needed for the cat to feel comfortable will vary depending on the temperament of the children and the cat.

Pick a quiet time to introduce the cat to children and let the cat approach whenever he is ready. Encourage play sessions between the cat and children, but let the children know that the cat is not a toy, and when he walks away it's a message he has had enough for the time being. Running away is a cat's defense mechanism; it says he is no longer enjoying the situation. If, out of enthusiasm, the children try to constrain the cat or force him to continue with the game, the cat will in most cases react by scratching and biting. Always supervise young children and cats, so you can read the cat's signals and ensure that playtime remains a fun activity for both.

No. 3 CAT SENSE

FELINE INTERACTION WITH THEIR ENVIRONMENT

*"It always gives me a shiver
when I see a cat seeing what I can't see."*
—Eleanor Farjeon, author

*L*ike people, felines see, smell, hear, touch, and taste. Their senses, for the most part, are much more highly developed than ours. People have about five million odor-sensitive cells in their noses, while cats have approximately 200 million. Cats need only one-fifth of the light people do to see at night, and they can hear sounds approximately four times farther away than humans. All this is very impressive, as is the wonderful engineering feat that is their whiskers.

An understanding of the ways in which our felines use their senses to interact with the environment helps us to understand them, and why they act as they do. It also strongly reinforces a cat reality: felines are predatory. They may be domesticated, but cats remain hunters. It is not something they do to amuse themselves; it's who they are and what they were made to do.

EYES AND VISION

It is often said that cats can see in the dark, but they can't, no more than we can. This misunderstanding may be based on two facts: 1) when their vision is impaired their other senses kick in to guide them; and 2) what may seem pitch dark to us does not appear so to our cats. Their eyes are built for the dark, with a layer of cells beneath their retinas

Cats and Television

As most cat-owners can attest, cats love to watch television. This is due to the way the television signal is displayed, which results in our predatory feline hunters—who are experts at spotting motion—seeing movement from the screen that we can't. This may also explain why cats can appear captivated by something that their human counterparts are unable to detect, whether it is a small spider slowly crawling or a bird perched in a tree at. No wonder then that they were initially domesticated to hunt pests that would otherwise have been able to move around undetected.

THE EXTRA SENSE

The Jacobson (or vomeronasal) organ gives cats the ability to "taste" scent. This helps cats to examine the scents of other animals to know how recently they were there and if they are foe, prey, or possible mate. The flehmen response—when the cat grimaces with lips curled and mouth open—precipitates this analysis, because it is through that response that scent molecules are drawn in to the top of the cat's mouth, where the Jacobson organ is located.

that collects and reflects light. In dim light, cats will fully dilate their pupils, so as to take advantage of the maximum available light. This enables them to see in conditions that are impossible for us, and these light-reflecting cells also give cats the glow-in-the-dark eye appearance they are known for. Their forward-facing eyes provide the excellent depth perception predators need in order to know just the right moment to strike at prey and, because of rods in their retina that act as motion detectors, cats discern form and movement easily. A cat's eyes are the eyes of a nocturnal hunter, providing everything they need to be successful. This comes at the expense of visual acuity—the ability to distinguish separate objects—and peripheral vision. Despite their very large eyes, cats, like humans, have to turn their heads to see anything that is not in front of them.

Since their eyes maximize any available light, full sun can be too much for a cat. To combat this, cats contract their pupils to a slit when needed, in order to restrict the amount of light to their retina. They can still see very well with their contracted pupils; in fact, the only times cats don't see well is when it comes to color. They are not color-blind as once was thought, but their need to distinguish color is little and their ability limited.

SMELL AND TASTE

Kittens are blind at birth, and they rely on scent to locate their mothers so they can feed. It is one of the first senses they use, and it remains important all of their life. Scent allows them to communicate with other felines, sniff out trouble, and learn about the world around them. Male cats mark their territory with urine or use the scent glands in their face and feet to leave pheromones that send a message to other felines. Unspayed females use these scent markings to select a mate, while males either respect the territorial message left, or leave their own scent markings to communicate a challenge. Sniffing at scent markings tells our felines who was there, and what their intention was: friend or foe. A cat's sense of smell is approximately 14 times stronger than that of a human's, meaning a litter box that may smell slightly to us will be overwhelming to our felines who possess much larger nasal organs.

⊛ Cat Fact

A cat's sense of smell is strongest in the evening, as befits a nocturnal hunter, because it is at this time that the air temperature is lower than the ground temperature.

PREDATOR VERSUS PREY

The anatomy of a cat is specific to that of a predator, from their sight, hearing, and sense of touch and smell. One example: Excellent depth perception and distance judgment are needed for a hunter to time jumps and leaps at prey, and a cat's forward-facing eyes and binocular vision facilitate this. Conversely, prey—such as birds—typically have eyes at the side of their heads. They don't need to turn their heads to change their visual relationship to something, and this peripheral vision helps them spot danger.

Scent is so integral to cats that they have special organs at the top of their mouth, known as the Jacobson or vomeronasal organs. The flehmen response—when the cat curls back his lips and seems to grimace with his mouth open—sends pheromones and other scents to the Jacobson organ, through which cats are able to analyze scent molecules inhaled through their mouth, rather than relying on nose alone. A cat's sense of taste is closely related to scent, which helps him decide whether something is worth tasting in the first place. Cats can distinguish between salty, bitter, sour, and sweet, and prefer the first three. Most cats will avoid sweet-tasting food or, if they eat it, suffer indigestion as a result.

EARS AND HEARING

Cats can hear at a wider range of frequencies than a human can, and at a distance approximately four times farther. Their ears are large in relation to their head size and better designed to capture sound. Highly mobile, their ears rotate to capture sound more accurately, and they can distinguish even the slightest variances in sound, enabling them to determine much about their prey before they see it. They hear better when still, which is why you will often see them pause while their ears twitch to pinpoint the sound's location, at which point the cat resumes movement. A feline's ears are impressive, but they contribute to more than superior hearing. Located in the inner ear is the vestibular apparatus, responsible for a cat's excellent sense of balance.

🐾 Cat Fact

A cat's ears pivot toward sound to capture it and pinpoint its location, which studies have shown they are able to do from up to three feet away in less than a second.

into your cat's skin—although they do fall out occasionally, only to be replaced—and they exist on the cat's body (carpal vibrissae) and face (facial vibrissae). Nerve endings attached to the shaft base of the whiskers recognize shifts in air movement and provide sensory feedback to the cat, which helps cats to navigate easily, even at night. These message-carrying nerves receive information from the touch receptors in a cat's whiskers, skin, and coat that keep felines directly connected to what is going on around them at all times. This is because air currents change depending on where people, animals, or objects are, and the very sensitive feline whiskers detect these directional changes, providing constant and up-to-date information to the cat.

TOUCH

The skin of our cats is covered in touch receptors, as is their coat. Hairs, known as tylotrichs, are interspersed within the coat and these recognize pressure and air currents. The feline nose and paw pads are also covered with touch receptors. They are even more sensitive since, without a covering of hair, they are very responsive to temperature.

Cats are known to be fast on their feet, graceful, and very quick to react, and their whiskers facilitate this. So much more than decorative, the sensory properties of whiskers result in a very sophisticated feline sense of touch. Whiskers are long, thick, and flexible, and two to three times thicker than your cat's regular hair. They are embedded deep

⊛ Cat Fact

Air currents change as they move around people, animals, and objects. Cats are sensitive to these changes, which provide the cat with a regular news update as to what is going on in his environment.

The placement of the whiskers is not random, and each plays its role in helping the cat navigate. The whiskers on the underside of the forelegs (carpal vibrissae) help cats feel for prey and judge distances when leaping. The whiskers above a cat's eyes, known as superciliary, and the cheek whiskers, known as genal, act as an early warning signal if anything gets too close to the eyes, blinking if touched to protect

the eyes from injury. The whiskers that first come to mind when you think of a cat—the thick and longer muzzle whiskers, known as mystacials—work the hardest. These muzzle whiskers are generally as long as the cat's body width and their tips are very sensitive—perfect indicators of space for the cat that sticks his head into an opening to investigate whether he will fit.

PHYSICAL CONTACT

Every cat is different; however, figuring out the physical contact your cat most enjoys is not difficult, as he will quickly let you know! You can also follow the example of cats in the wild, who nuzzle and groom each other under the chin, behind the ears, and down the spine to the base of the tail. These remain the areas most cats enjoy to be petted, whereas bellies, tails, and feet are generally no-go zones.

⊛ Cat Fact

The sensitivity of a cat's whiskers is so great that they can detect even the slightest directional change in the air, enabling cats to react quickly and navigate surroundings even when sight-impaired.

A cat's whiskers are mobile and are pushed back when they are in the way, such as when fighting or eating. They sweep forward when needed to investigate something, for example, at night when they help cats to "see" in the dark. They are also used to compensate for the poor vision cats have when viewing things close up. Although experts at distance viewing, cats are less skilled at seeing what is directly beneath their nose, such as the mouse or bird they have captured. Muzzle whiskers investigate and tell them if the prey is alive or not, and their chin and lip, or mandibular, whiskers give them precise directions as to where to place the bite that will finish the prey off if needed.

More Than Just Good Looks

Cats can function without their whiskers, but you may notice them bumping into things and, until their whiskers grow back, they will be at a disadvantage. Their sense of touch is compromised, which lessens their ability to judge distances, move around easily, and hunt. Whiskers perform an important function and should not be trimmed or cut; they are part of what makes a cat a cat.

No. 4 FELINE PHYSICAL COMMUNICATION

FACIAL EXPRESSIONS AND BODY LANGUAGE

"The problem with cats
is that they get the exact same look
whether they see a moth or an axe-murderer."
—Paula Poundstone, comedian

C ats are often described as inscrutable—until you really get to know them, that is. When you understand the meaning behind their physical messages, you realize that they are regularly communicating their mood and intentions through their primary vocabulary of facial expressions and body language. Once you are able to read the signs, and understand the cues that tell you if they are relaxed, happy, fearful, or aggressive, your communication with your cat is enhanced and your bond is strengthened.

As solitary animals, cats do not have the same breadth of body language that pack animals do. They never needed an extensive vocabulary as, unlike dogs, wild cats did not depend on each other for survival. The communication that grew out of pack behavior, such as appeasement signaling between dogs, was not necessary and so never became part of the feline vocabulary. The visual cues cats do use, however—while not as extensive as those dogs use—are easily understood by other felines, and by people once we understand the physical language of cats. Some messages are more straightforward to translate than others. For example, when a cat's spine is arched in a parody of a witch's cat, it is typically understood to mean that all is not well, and that the cat may be ready to strike. Ears that are swiveled and angled to the side, however, may not be as easily recognized as a sign of aggression.

🐾 Cat Fact

Dogs and cats communicate differently. A wagging tail is the sign of a happy dog, while a cat's moving tail may signal agitation or aggression.

THE BIG PICTURE

Some actions can be difficult to translate accurately if looked at in isolation. A cat can communicate fear or aggression by tucking his tail low or by a puffed tail held high, but a tail standing tall can also indicate excitement. How do you know if you are interpreting your cat's message correctly? Look at the big picture, and how your cat combines cues to send a message.

CONFIDENT AGGRESSION: The cat's gaze is fixed and intense, with pupils constricted to slits. Ears are erect and facing forward, or with the ears folded so that the backs are clearly visible. The cat's tail will be low, and he will either walk directly toward his opponent or approach him with an exaggerated sideways motion meant to make him look bigger and more intimidating.

ALERT: Ears are erect and rotate so as to capture the sound of anything approaching, whether friend or foe. Pupils are dilated so as to extend their field of vision, and when something of interest is spotted ears and whiskers will be forward-facing.

FEARFUL AGGRESSION: Spine will be arched with hackles raised and tail erect. Teeth will be barred to intimidate, and ears will be back in the defensive, protective mode. Gaze will be intense and focused, claws may be extended, and the cat will look ready to pounce.

LISTEN AND LOOK

A cat's ears are mobile and as such are capable of communicating much depending on their position: forward and erect, flattened and facing back or forward, or swiveled to the side. When both ears are erect and forward-pointing, the cat is signaling alertness, in the same way a person might lean forward to see something that has caught their attention. One ear forward and one ear back is a mixed message that says the cat could go either way. Ambivalent at the moment, this could progress to both ears forward or back. The latter signals defensiveness; the cat has tucked his ears back to protect them from what might come next. If the cat's ears have folded so that their backs can be seen from the front this communicates aggression, and that the cat is ready to attack. Ears swiveled to the side also mean business, and are the ears of a cat who feels threatened and will pounce first to protect himself. Ears that twitch signal nervousness, which may progress to flattened ears, unless the potential threat is lessened. Your cat's eyes can tell you a lot about his current mood and intentions, particularly his pupils and the intensity of his gaze. Cats need only one-fifth of the light that we do to see, which is why they see so much better than us in dim light and why full light can dazzle them. They dilate their pupils to make the most of the available light at night, and constrict their pupils to slits in the full light of day to restrict the amount of light reaching their retinas. That is normal. However, if your cat's eyes are dilated during the day you should pay attention. A fearful cat's pupils will appear larger than normal, an instinctive reaction that provides the cat with a wider field of vision. This allows them to see more of their surroundings and possible danger. An angry or dominant cat will do the opposite. His eyes will be slits but, just as in the fearful cat, his gaze will be intensely focused.

Marking Territory

When a cat rubs his face against objects this is known as bunting, and it is the cat's way of leaving his scent to mark territory. Furniture scratching is also a way of marking territory with scent, with the added benefit—to the cat—of leaving a visual cue as well. The more anxious a cat becomes about his territory, for example, after a move or when a new cat is introduced to the home, the more his scent and visual marking behavior will increase.

🐾 Cat Fact

The facial expressions of a cat indicate mood, but this is secondary, a result of the functional advantage (and primary reason) for the change in expression. Widened eyes with dilated pupils are indicators of a frightened cat, but their practical application is to provide a wider field of vision for a cat to scan for danger.

MOUTH AND MUZZLE WHISKERS

The cat's reputation for being hard to read is partly a result of his minimal facial expressions, particularly when it comes to using his mouth. It is generally kept closed, although visible teeth may signal aggression, and a yawn can communicate stress or be an offensive signal. A cat's muzzle whiskers also communicate. Pushed forward, they show curiosity or contentment, while whiskers pushed back can signal defensiveness; the cat is getting ready to fight but protecting his whiskers beforehand by sweeping them into a back position.

TAILS TRANSLATED

Tail position and movement are telling, and can be one of the first ways that new owners begin to understand their cat's language, and therefore bond with their feline. A tail tucked low, a tail puffed up, or a tail that moves in wide arcs can all communicate fear or aggression. A tail held high communicates confidence and if it gently waves it may signal excitement, whether in greeting or due to anticipation. More agitated tail motion can signal anxiety or aggression, and a twitching tail communicates that the cat is in predatory mode.

🐾 Cat Fact

A cat's response to stimuli is generally an instinctive reaction. Fear and anger typically elicit the same response: aggressive behavior.

Aggression

Cats are not normally aggressive by nature, but even the most easy-going cat can exhibit aggressive behavior if they are scared or angry. Cats do not like to be constrained or roughly handled, and can lash out with claws or teeth if they feel trapped or mistreated. Watch out for any of these signs: flattened ears, extended claws, raised hackles. The cat may stare at its aggressor from slit-like pupils or be wide-eyed, scanning for threats, and teeth may be barred. Give an aggressive cat space, particularly from children who may not understand that the cat has had enough and no longer wants to play.

then he is prepared to defend himself. A dominant aggressive cat does not wait to take his cues from others. He will walk directly toward the animal or person that poses a threat, with his eyes fixed on them, and his rear legs will typically be stiff. Or, he will approach with an exaggerated sideways walk, meant to make him look larger. His body language tells you that when threatened this cat is not afraid to react with aggression, and he will act offensively.

The message your cat sends out through his coat is easy to read: a bristled, standing-up coat means something is wrong. Your cat is scared or angry and his raised hackles are meant to make him look bigger than he is, a typical defensive/offensive body language pose meant to intimidate so the threat retreats, or to serve as warning.

BODY POSTURE AND COAT TALES

Your cat's posture also sends a message, particularly when he feels threatened. In those situations he will react with aggressive fear or anger, both messages that should be heeded. An arched back is triggered by fear and is an instinctive reaction. It is meant to intimidate, by making the cat look bigger in an attempt to repel the person or animal he feels threatened by.

A fearful cat may lean away from the potential threat, with his claws extended in readiness just in case. His head may be tilted to the side and his gaze intense. This is the body posture and actions of a cat who would prefer not to fight. He would rather the subject of his anxiety retreat, but if it doesn't

⊗ *Cat Fact*

A cat in a confrontation will show stress through the action of his pupils dilating/getting larger and constricting/getting smaller.

MIXED MESSAGES

Cats that are unable to communicate through the physical cues recognized by other felines are at a disadvantage. This would include cats who have had their whiskers trimmed or removed, and breeds like the American Curl and the Scottish Fold, who cannot move their ears as other cats do. Not only is their communication affected, they are also at risk from other felines who misread them. The ears of the Scottish Fold are permanently distorted back, which can be interpreted by other cats as signaling aggression, while the American Curl's ears are permanently flattened, which can give off an unintentional defensive message.

No. 5 FELINE VOCAL COMMUNICATION

THE MEANING BEHIND THE SOUND

"Cats speak a subtle language in which few sounds carry many meanings, depending on how they are sung or purred. 'Mnrhnh' means comfortable soft chairs. It also means fish. It means genial companionship ... and the absence of dogs."

—Val Schaffner, author

Cats use vocalization most often with humans, because they have learned it gets a response. Domestication and close contact with humans has led to increased vocalization, whereas in the wild adult cats rarely "speak" and, like the cat-to-cat chats between domesticated felines, communicate primarily through body language and scent.

Some cats are more vocal than others. The Siamese and Oriental breeds are known to "talk" more, while other breeds, like the Russian Blue and the American and British Shorthair, are typically silent. Common vocalizations used by felines include the meow, purr, growl, hiss, and chatter, with each having many possible meanings depending on when and where they are used. Meaning is further translated by taking into consideration the facial expression, body language, tone, and volume at which the sound is delivered.

In Good Company

It is not only our domestic cats that purr; in fact, the number and sheer range of creatures that purr may come as quite a surprise. From large animals such as elephants and gorillas to considerably smaller ones, such as rabbits and raccoons—they are all said to purr. The house cat's more fearsome relatives in the wild, such as lions and pumas, unsurprisingly also share this trait, although it is fair to assume that what is endearing in your family cat is rather more intimidating in the cats of the wild.

Cat Fact

Some cats have a wider vocabulary than others, which can be a result of genetics, personality, and need.

1. THE MEOW

WHAT YOU HEAR:

The meow is onomatopoeic, with its name imitating its sound. It varies in length and pitch, rhythm, volume, and pronunciation, depending on the individual cat and on the message.

WHAT IT MEANS:

Meows are attention-seeking, and are used to communicate greetings, complaints, and demands. In the latter case, the typical meow says "I want," and as cat owners get to know their feline they begin to understand the variances used to communicate, "I want to go out," or "I want food." It is a multi-faceted vocalization. The lower the sound, the more anxious the cat is; for example, the plaintive hungry meow. The more high-toned it is the happier the cat typically is; for example, the welcome meow. A falling cadence indicates protest or a complaint; a lilting cadence is usually used in greeting; while a short, sharp meow may communicate displeasure.

WHAT TO KNOW:

Kittens use the meow to communicate with their mother and littermates, but as they age they rarely use this sound with adult cats, reserving its use for their communication with people. The best way of figuring out what your cat means by a meow is through observation. Look at the situation in which the meow is used, and the accompanying body language.

🐾 Cat Fact

In Egypt the cat is known by the name "miw," in China by "maow," and in Thailand by "maa-oh" or "meo," just like the sound most commonly associated with our felines.

2. THE PURR

WHAT YOU HEAR:
The purr is a tonal buzzing; a rhythmic, vibrating, close-mouthed sound. Volume and tone varies from cat to cat.

WHAT IT MEANS:
Generally a purr communicates contentment and invites affectionate contact through petting and stroking. It can also be used to self-comfort or in self-healing, as heard in cats that have been injured or are sick. Cats may also purr in anticipation, for example, when they hear the familiar noises that precede feeding.

WHAT TO KNOW:
The purr is an enigma. Researchers differ as to the explanation, generally agreeing that like all cat vocalizations there are many interpretations. Most cat owners would be in agreement that cats purr when they are content. Although this is true, studies have shown that in the wild it is also used to comfort and reassure. Mother cats may purr when returning from the hunt, to make contact with their kittens without alerting predators. Cats also use it to calm their kittens and keep them together in the nest. Felines purr during inhalation or exhalation, when the muscles in their voicebox vibrate. Ongoing studies indicate that endorphins may be released through the action of purring, and that the quiet vibration of this vocalization may promote healing.

3. THE GROWL OR HISS

WHAT YOU HEAR:
A throaty vocalization, typically low in tone but of high intensity.

WHAT IT MEANS:
The growl and hiss are both used to communicate fear, anger, or annoyance. When fear-based it is used to repel threats; when used in annoyance or anger it gives warning of aggressive behavior.

WHAT TO KNOW:
Often accompanied by a head drawn back, eyes opened wide with dilated pupils, and flattened ears. This cat is prepared to defend itself, and its warning should be heeded. The growl or hiss is a precursor to aggression, and if not listened to the cat will proceed to communicate "go away" through his claws and teeth.

4. THE CHATTER

WHAT YOU HEAR:
The chatter is the sound of a cat's teeth or jaw clicking together.

WHAT IT MEANS:
It is generally thought to express excitement, as it is often used when the cat is observing prey. Some experts believe that it is meant to reassure prey, while others are of the opinion that it may be meant as a threatening sound. It may also be used out of frustration due to out-of-reach prey; for example, a bird the cat sees through a window.

WHAT TO KNOW:
Like most cat vocalizations, there is debate surrounding the reflexive chattering noise a cat makes. Some look to the cat's predator instincts, and posit that this is rehearsal behavior, in anticipation of a successful hunt and to practice the killing bite to be delivered to prey.

One form of vocalization that employs a higher tone is the trill. This is a closed-mouth murmur, often used by the cat to acknowledge the presence or actions of another. An offshoot of the purr, it is often accompanied by an arched back—reminiscent of a stretch rather than a parody of a Halloween cat—that is most often translated as a friendly feline greeting and invitation to approach.

Interestingly, many cats go through their lives without vocalizing until something triggers the use of sound. They may still mouth the "meow," although silently. This could be due to an upper respiratory disease or a growth that makes vocalization difficult, or it may have nothing to do with a medical condition. It may simply be triggered by distance, for example, when you are in sight but out of range.

Catty Behavior

Angry or fearful hissing or growling is most often directed at other felines and will usually be the product of a territorial dispute. This sort of confrontation is unsurprising given the increasingly tight space we are introducing domesticated cats into. It is less common for cats to display that behavior toward people; one possible scenario for provoking it may be that the cat feels threatened, constrained, or mistreated by a human.

🐾 Cat Fact

Although an instinctive behavior, vocalization is also learned. Cats work out that their people respond to sound, thus reinforcing the behavior.

FELINE TO FELINE

INTERACTION WITH OTHER CATS

*"When a cat chooses to be friendly, it's
a big deal, because a cat is picky."*
—Mike Deupree, author

*N*ot only can many felines be picky, they are
independent animals. Although they can be friendly
and affectionate with other felines, they are not
social in the same inherent way that dogs are. They are also
fiercely territorial, which is what much cat-to-cat chat is about,
communicated primarily through scent and body language.

Your cat's scent is his calling card, used to send messages to other felines. It communicates much, from sexual status to—very importantly—territorial claims. In the wild, territory was a matter of food; the scarcer the supply, the larger the territory. Domesticated cats may not need to worry about their next meal, but are still fiercely territorial. If your cat has access to the outside he will sniff at trees in the yard and garden to receive messages from felines who have been there; he may regularly spray, even indoors at times; or exhibit clawing, rubbing, and chinning behavior to communicate through scent with other felines.

Cat Fact

Unlike dogs, there is not a hierarchy for felines to be concerned with, but they are fiercely concerned with territory.

1. SPRAYING

WHAT YOU SEE:
Your cat may be patrolling his territory—the garden, yard, or inside your home—when he backs up against a wall, tree, door, or furniture, and releases urine backwards against his chosen object. His tail will be erect and quivering, and he will be standing tall with his rump high.

WHAT IT MEANS:
Urine marks alert other cats to the presence of the marking cat. The cat exhibiting the spraying behavior is marking his territory with the scent of his urine, to announce he was there and to claim ownership of that area.

BEHIND THE SIGNS

Indoor Spraying

Cats do not normally spray indoors as the home represents security, and there is no need to send messages to other cats. If, however, it is a multi-cat household or there has been a recent upheaval, such as a move to a new home, then felines may feel the need to lay claim to territory through indoor spraying. Interestingly, studies have shown that urine spraying indoors generally increases in proportion to the number of cats in the home.

WHAT TO KNOW:

Spraying, particularly when it is indoors, is sometimes confused with soiling, but when cats urinate they crouch. The latter involves discharging urine to release pressure on the bladder, while spraying may involve only a small amount of urine with a primary purpose of releasing scent. Some cat owners never encounter this behavior, while others see it intermittently. Spraying may increase if there have been changes to the household, such as a move to a new home. This increase may be done out of anxiety or fear of the change, and an effort to lay claim to a new area. When a new cat moves into an area, they typically either have to fight it out with the existing cats of the street or agree by mutual consent on territory and right of passage, and the same is true for indoor felines of a multi-cat household. Cats that have been neutered generally exhibit less spraying behavior.

2. CLAWING

WHAT YOU SEE:
Your cat uses his claws to leave visible scratch marks on trees, furniture, or doors.

WHAT IT MEANS:
Visually through the scratch marks, and olfactorily through the pheromones released by scratching, your cat is leaving a territorial message. If this clawing is done in front of another cat some believe this is also a dominant, or warning gesture.

WHAT TO KNOW:
Felines sweat through their paws and there are also scent glands located there. Clawing as a form of communication is done to deposit the secretions from these glands, to send scent and visual messages to other felines. In multi-cat households where the scratching is indoors and widespread then the clawing is typically a form of territorial communication among the resident felines. In this case, the best defense against clawing is to make the cat exhibiting the behavior feel safe and secure in his environment. In multi-cat households, provide high resting places throughout the home, areas the cats can individually use to get

away; provide multiple litter boxes, sleeping areas, and food and water bowls, so any territorial squabbling over these is reduced. If the territorial challenge comes from felines outside the home, you may want to block the cat flap and provide access to outside on demand. The latter situation is definitely harder to solve, and a feline behaviorist may be necessary to analyze the specific situation.

⊛ Cat Fact

Sometimes clawing is not done to send a message but to maintain claws. In this case, regular trimming and the introduction of a scratching post can help.

CATFIGHTS

A "catfight" is a term sometimes used to describe a fight among humans, characterized by scratching. However, as any cat owner who has witnessed a fight between felines can attest, a catfight can get much more involved than this. When cats fight—whether over territorial challenges or for any other reason—one cat is usually the aggressor who initiates. He will typically walk directly up to the other cat or approach him in a swaying sideways walk and boldly sniff the other's tail, all signs of confident aggression. The other cat, as defender, may react with fearful aggression, leaning back and away, but still ready to fight if needed. Dogs have physical cues to express appeasement to other canines. They are able to communicate, "I'm not a threat and I recognize your dominance," which is necessary messaging for such social and hierarchy-focused animals. Cats do not have this same vocabulary. As a result, fights can be violent, but generally the aggressor will recognize the defender's body language as fearful, and may decide that his challenge has been won and there is no need for further aggressive behavior.

✿ Cat Fact

Cats that know each other well may touch noses. They may lick the other cat's coat to communicate affection and strengthen their bond by grooming the other cat.

Affection Between Felines

A sign of mutual acceptance between felines is allowing the other to sniff beneath their tail. When friendly with another cat, felines may show their affection and trust by sleeping side by side, sitting close to one another, and grooming each other. A greeting marked with fluttering blinking eyes or a yawn also signals friendly feeling. Cats comfortable with each other may exchange facial pheromones through cheek rubbing.

BODY LANGUAGE

The body language of cats, covered in Chapter 4, is easily understood by other felines. Although independent animals, unlike the social and pack-oriented canine, felines do communicate with each other through expression and physical cues. Cats will use their eyes to communicate, whether through an aggressive stare of unmistakable animosity, or with a quick eye-blinking greeting that can signal affection. Eyes wide open are wary and watchful, on the alert and ready for aggressive action if necessary, while semi-closed eyes show trust. In cats that are friendly and familiar this may progress to grooming each other, a further sign of trust and affection. A threat is communicated through a stiff body, head usually low but with eyes focused and intense, and the rump elevated. This tells the other feline, "stay away," whereas a relaxed posture and a tail that is erect and curved says, "let's play."

Cat Fact

When cats have been properly socialized to other cats from a young age they communicate with other felines better, and understand the significance of the other's body language.

Litter Box Communication

In multi-cat households, feuding cats may take their fight to the litter box. Cats are normally fastidious creatures who bury their droppings but, if there are problems between the two cats, droppings may be left out as a not-so-friendly message to the other feline, marking territory and making it clear which areas belong to which cat.

Leaving scent deposits is reassuring and helps a cat feel confident in his surroundings. When challenged by other felines, however, the cat may lose his swagger. In a multi-cat household he may stick close to certain areas while avoiding others, or, if the challenge comes from outside, an indoor/outdoor cat may change his behavior to remain inside more frequently.

🐾 Cat Fact

Cats do not have signals of submission as dogs do, but in a fight an aggressive cat will recognize when the other cat is defending himself, rather than provoking a fight, and back off.

BUNTING

Cats also communicate through scent by "bunting," rubbing against an object with their forehead, cheeks, or chin. When they do so they are leaving secretions from the sebaceous scent glands located in the face. This behavior is sometimes translated as an affectionate gesture; however, rubbing with the chin is usually reserved for territorial marking.

CAT TO PEOPLE

THE FELINE AND HUMAN BOND

"The cat does not offer services. The cat offers itself. Of course he wants care and shelter. You don't buy love for nothing. Like all pure creatures, cats are practical."
—William S. Burroughs, author

*C*ats in ancient Egypt were worshipped as gods, and breeds such as the elegant Abyssinian were celebrated in the artwork of that time. Felines of the new world had a different experience. Prior to 1870, cats were valued for their superior mousing ability—with the British Shorthair apparently traveling on the Mayflower for that express purpose—but their relationship with humans was limited. It is only in the last 150 years that cats have become accepted and cherished as pets worldwide. Today, most cat owners consider their feline to be part of the family.

The bond between cats and people has been proven regardless of when the particular feline and human form an alliance. Those fortunate to share their home with a cat from its first months as a kitten and onward form a strong bond, but so too do those who meet their feline when he is an adult or senior cat. The relationship is symbiotic, and very different from the relationship people have with other pets. Tropical fish may be loved for their shape and color, but although there is an appreciation for their beauty there is not a bond. Dogs bond with their people, but it is a relationship rooted in pack behavior and hierarchy, with one leading and the other following. The relationship with our felines is different. They do not recognize us as alpha, or take a subordinate role in the household. As cat owners know all too well, our cats listen to us only when they feel like it.

The bond is strong nonetheless, perhaps because cat owners tend to worship their cats as the ancient Egyptians did—a situation that cats graciously accept.

🐾 Cat Fact

Studies have shown that one of the reasons behind the feline–human bond is that our cats, like canines, are animals of sufficient size and response to forge ties. The iguana may make a great pet, but not necessarily a companionable one in the way that felines are.

DIFFERENT STROKES FOR DIFFERENT CATS

Cats, like people, can be aloof or gregarious. Regardless of their personality, both are capable of strong bonding; they just show their affection and trust differently. Some, like the Maine Coon, will be demonstrably lovable and affectionate. Others, like the Russian Blue, may appear shy at first, until they get to know you. The Siamese and the Oriental, for example, want to be part of everything you do, while the Persian enjoys your company but is generally just as happy watching the goings-on of the house from the sofa. Every cat is unique, regardless of breed or pedigree, and your bond with them will be unique, based on the personalities of those involved: you and your feline.

BEHIND THE SIGNS

You're Mine

Cats typically mark their territory by rubbing their head on it, in a process known as "bunting." This releases pheromones from the sebaceous glands in their face and deposits their scent on the object or surface they have rubbed up against, claiming it as their own. This territorial gesture extends to a cat's people and is translated as an affectionate gesture; by doing so, your cat is laying claim to you. They will do this to other cats as well.

Cat Fact

Kittens benefit from remaining with their mothers for the first eight weeks of their life. If they are handled gently for short periods of time daily during that period, they are better able to adapt to people, and bond more quickly.

BONDING 101

If you get your cat as a kitten, give him a name that is one or two syllables, to make it easier for him to recognize, and—in the case of two-syllable names—to differentiate it from the typically one-syllable training commands you may teach your feline. Use the name consistently when addressing your cat so he learns to respond to it. Socialize your kitten early, introducing him to other people, pets, and new experiences, making sure that each socialization exercise is a positive one. This helps your cat get to know his world and be comfortable in it. Although fearful behavior is in part genetic, it is enhanced through lack of socialization. It is lessened by positive exposure to cars, a vacuum, children, dogs, regular handling,

🐾 *Cat Fact*

Some cats may be predisposed to standoffish behavior, but the more time we spend in close contact with them the friendlier they become, as long as they are not rushed and are allowed to initiate the contact.

and anything or anyone else your cat may encounter in his life. Once he knows he has nothing to fear from them he is a more confident and well-balanced feline,

Cupboard Love?

Many adult cats often act like kittens with their people. Perhaps they don't have the same energy that they once did, but they will communicate to their humans with a meow, a vocalization reserved in the wild for kittens speaking to their mothers. They will also sit on our laps, receiving the same warmth that their mothers once provided. In part, this is reinforced through our role in providing the food they eat. We have inadvertently taken on the role of mother and hunter, and they respond instinctively. This, however, as cat owners worldwide know, is only one aspect of the very rich relationship between cats and their people.

at ease in his world. Adult cats can also learn to get used to different experiences. The key in both cases is patience and consistency on the owner's part.

When meeting a new cat, let him approach you. When he is comfortable with you—and he will let you know by his body language and vocalizations—he may invite physical contact. He may approach you with his tail high, or he may arch his back in a relaxed manner and meow or trill. This is your invitation to pet and stroke him under his chin, behind his ears, and down along his spine to the base of his tail, but avoid his belly, tail, and feet if you want to remain on good terms. As you and your cat get into a routine, you will become more familiar, with both of you getting to know each other through observation. He may walk toward you in a relaxed manner to get your attention, or he may walk closely in front of you as if he wanted to trip you up—cat cue that it is feeding time. Or he may wrap himself around your legs as you are sitting, signaling that it is time for attention or dinner. Just as with any relationship, proximity brings insight into the other. You will begin to understand his language, just as he will begin to understand yours.

No. 8 LONE HUNTERS

INSIGHT INTO WHAT MAKES A CAT A CAT

"Prowling his own quiet backyard or asleep by the fire, he is still only a whisker away from the wilds."

—Jean Burden, author

Descended from the wild cat, our domestic felines retain the inherent hunting prowess of their ancestors. Expert stalkers, they move slowly at first, just as the cheetah and tiger do. They fix prey in their sight and silently go after it, rushing and leaping when they judge the time is right, then finish the prey off with a killing bite of precision.

Inherited Behavior

The larger members of the cat family that our felines are descended from may have stalked bigger prey than the birds and rodents our domestic cats stalk, but their hunting behavior is the same: solitary and by stealth. They are extremely patient hunters and will be content to lie in wait for long periods, until the prey complacently puts a foot wrong. Their excellent vision and remarkable agility help them to capitalize on a moment's weakness. The next time you see your cat crouching almost perfectly still in the garden, you can be fairly confident they are on the hunt.

Our cat's anatomy and senses are designed to hunt. Teeth powerful enough to cut like scissors, claws that can be extended for traction while on the chase, eyes seemingly designed for nocturnal vision, whiskers as navigational devices— all these and more combine to make our cats the skilled hunters they are. Kittens practice hunting behavior from an early age through their play. It teaches them how to stalk and capture toys in the living room, and eventually prey in the wild.

To aid them in their hunt, cats have evolved as sprinters. They walk on their toes to facilitate quick take-offs and during the sprint their pliable muscles and flexible spine help to extend their stride. They excel at jumping and are able to leap up or across distances up to six times their own body length.

🐾 Cat Fact

Strength in their legs and back muscles are pivotal for successful leaping. Cats place their weight in their hindquarters when jumping, and this is what propels them up or forward.

BUILT FOR HUNTING

Ears: Mobile ears designed for directional hearing allow felines to move each ear independently, or together to listen for prey. Their ears face back to listen for anything approaching from behind or can swivel to the side and point forward when needed. They are designed to capture sound, and can hear a wider range of frequencies than humans can, and at a distance approximately four times farther. Their hearing is so sensitive that cats are able to hear the ultrasonic calls of rodent prey. Located in the inner ear is the vestibular apparatus, which contributes to the cat's superior sense of balance, so necessary when climbing, running, and leaping.

Active and Passive Hunting

There are two hunting strategies employed by cats. They actively stalk their prey, which is the behavior most commonly associated with our felines, or they wait in ambush for their prey to come to them, usually in cases where the prey lives in underground burrows. Cats also use height to observe their territory, leaping on prey from their high perch.

GIFTS FROM THE HUNT

There are differing theories as to why cats present the spoils of the hunt to their human family. Anthropologist Desmond Morris suggests that this behavior is meant to feed the less able members of their group—the humans—and to teach people to hunt by bringing them prey so they can refine their skills. Ethologist Paul Leyhausen suggests that cats recognize humans as part of their social group, and thus bring the kill home to the "nest" just as wild cats do.

If your cat is an avid hunter and "gift" giver, you can lessen the frequency of him bringing prey home by putting bells on his collar that will alert prey to his presence, although many cats figure this out quickly, and hold their necks still so they don't make a sound. You may also want to keep your cat in at night, or when his hunting is most prolific. Never punish your cat for hunting. He will not make the connection, as he is only doing what is natural.

Eyes: The eyes of our felines contract or dilate as needed for better visibility, depending on light conditions. At night, their pupils are dilated and the tapetum, the reflective layer behind a cat's retina, works to capture available light, facilitating the superior night vision needed for nocturnal hunters.

Nose: With a sense of smell approximately 14 times stronger than that of humans, cats can sniff out prey at a distance.

🐾 Cat Fact

Cats have binocular vision: both eyes are used together, they are able to detect faint objects, and they have superior depth perception.

Mouth: The jaw of the cat is hinged so that lateral movement is limited, which contributes to how precise and fierce their bite is when dealing with prey. Their teeth are those of a hunter, with the premolar and first molar—known as the carnassial pair—acting as scissors, perfect for the shearing of meat in the days when their dinners did not come out of a bag or tin. Those sharp spines on the tongue, known as papillae and felt by many owners when licked by their cat, are optimally designed to tear flesh from prey.

Whiskers: As people and animals move around, the air currents change. Our cats' whiskers are so sensitive they pick up on these changing currents, and the whiskers' nerve endings send sensory messages to the feline brain, providing navigational information that is put to good use in the hunt. Their foreleg whiskers sense currents that aid in judging distances when leaping, and through touch these whiskers also help cats feel for prey. Muzzle whiskers direct a cat who has caught prey to go in for the killing bite; their depth perception may be excellent, but a cat's vision close up is not, and he can't always see what is in front of his face.

Skin: The loose skin of felines means that they are able to turn their body to confront prey or predator, even when in their grip.

Spinal Column: Humans have five lumbar vertebrae and 12 thoracic vertebrae; our cats have seven and 13 respectively. This translates to enhanced spinal flexibility in our felines, which—when combined with the caudal vertebrae in their tails that contribute to balance when climbing or cornering during a chase—makes them mobile and fast on their feet, just as hunters should be.

Paws: As cats walk, they place each hind paw almost exactly where the corresponding forepaw was, leaving minimal tracks and a path for their hind legs to follow—especially useful in rough terrain as it contributes to their balance and speed.

Claws: Protractile claws can be extended all at once or per paw, depending on the cat's need: for traction when hunting, fighting, and prey catching. At other times, the claws are kept sheathed, which protects them from the wear and tear of rough terrain and helps keep them sharp.

⊛ Cat Fact

Cats often become airborne in mid-sprint, particularly when rounding corners, at which times their tail provides them with the necessary balance.

TERRITORY AND RANGE

INHERITED FELINE BEHAVIOR

"Always the cat remains a little beyond the limits we try to set for him in our blind folly."

—Andre Norton, author

A look at territory and range and what they mean to our felines provides a fascinating look into their world, and the language they use to defend it. Patrolling behavior, spraying, clawing, and bunting all suddenly make sense, and this insight helps us to better understand our felines, and take steps to lessen unwanted behaviors.

Cats are territorial and solitary animals. Although wild cats may form colonies, every feline, whether domestic house pet or feral cat, has an instinctive need for its own defined areas, their territory and their range. Although the terms are often used interchangeably, they have different meanings: territory is the area the cat will defend, and range is the area your cat inhabits. Domestic cats do not form colonies with neighboring cats, as feral cats might do. When domestic cats meet it is usually to assert their individual territorial rights.

Territory is generally smaller than range, and will be the area your cat rests in. Range size is generally a result of food supply: the more food available the smaller the range needs to be and vice versa. Although your cat does not need to worry about food supply his ancestors did. They relied entirely on their own ability to catch prey. If their hunting skills were impaired, for example, by other cats hunting their areas and the prey that resided there, they could not survive. Your domestic cat has no need to hunt for food but he still has an inherited need for territory and range, passed down from his wild ancestors. In multi-cat households, territory is established just as it is in the wild. Each cat will have its specific resting spots and if this territory is time-shared with other cats of the household then routines are typically followed, with each cat using it at a particular time of the day. Cats will patrol their territory and/or their range regularly, marking their area with their scent to leave a message for other felines by:

Clawing: scratching furniture, wallpaper, and doors inside the home and/or trees and fences outside.

Cat Fact

Studies have shown that the range of domestic cats is smaller than that of the wild cat, since domestic cats are fed at home and do not need to hunt to eat.

PROBLEM SCENT-MARKING

The most common reason that pet cats are put down or abandoned to shelters is because of problem spraying. Multi-cat households suffer most from this behavior, as well as from territory marking. If you are not breeding your cat then having your cat neutered is not only responsible cat ownership, it can also stop problem spraying. There are also pheromone sprays and diffusers available from pet supply stores that, when used in areas that your cat normally sprays, may prove effective, as might anti-anxiety medication prescribed by your veterinarian. Very important is removing the odor left by spraying, as it can trigger repeat performances. Specialty cleaning products are available, or a 50/50 white vinegar and water mix has also been found effective in some households. Ensure multiple sleeping areas, litter boxes, and food and water bowls, as it lessens the need for cats sharing their home with other felines to be territorial, which in turn can decrease both spraying and clawing behavior.

BEHIND THE SIGNS

Cat Fact

Scent-marking territory inside the home is generally only seen in multi-cat households when one feline challenges another cat's claim to the territory.

Litter Box Messages

In multi-cat households where territory claims are causing problems, cats may leave scent messages for the other cats by leaving their feces uncovered in the litter tray. This is not a normal feline behavior but, when needed, another way to send a territorial scent message.

Bunting: rubbing up against an object with their forehead, cheeks, and chin.

Spraying: depositing a small amount of urine on vertical surfaces, such as doors, walls, and furniture inside the home and/or fences and trees outside the home. Sweat and scent glands are located on the paws, and clawing releases these secretions onto the surface marked. Bunting accomplishes the same thing through the glands located in the face, and the strong-smelling pheromones in a cat's urine is just one more way to announce his presence to other cats.

Scent marking is a primary communication method for cats, providing information about the individual cat, such as age, health, sexual status, as well as when he was last there. These marks are scent signposts to other felines that, when unchallenged, result in that space being respected as another's area, at least on a time-share basis. Domestic cats with outside access establish their range. In females this may be the garden or yard, while male cats typically lay claim to a larger area, up to ten times that of the female range. The people of the home are recognized as part of that cat's group, but neighboring cats generally are not and so scent messages left outside are directed to them. The more familiar and trusting the cats become with each other, the less territorially they will act. If challenged, a cat's scent-marking behavior will typically increase.

Your cat's territory may include the radiator, fireplace, or window ledge, while his range may include the yard and surrounding area. Note where your cat rests at different times of the day over the course of a few days and you should see a pattern emerge that makes clear your cat's territory.

⊛ Cat Fact

Cats usually patrol their territory and range on a fixed schedule.

Air-Spraying

Cats that have been neutered generally do not spray, but if they are feeling anxious about their territory they may go through the motions of spraying. Although no urine is released they will back up against an object and stand tall with their rump and tail held high. There are different schools of thought as to whether neutering produces slight changes in a cat's behavior, including greater docility and dependency in females and increased aggression in males. Most experts agree that neutering will not change a cat's personality, but it can lessen or eliminate some unwanted hormone related problem behaviors.

SLEEP BEHAVIOR AND SIGNIFICANCE

"If there is one spot of sun spilling onto the floor, a cat will find it and soak it up."
—J. A. McIntosh, author

ats are so well known for their ability to nap at any time and in any place that the term "cat nap" has become common usage for describing the shortly snatched naps of humans. A look at the sleeping patterns of cats shows us how their behavior is influenced by their predatory natures and, even if the most hunting your cat does is stalking his toys, provides insight into what makes a cat a cat. Each cat is a mix of inherited traits along with their unique personalities, and an understanding of their sleep patterns helps us to better translate their behavior.

To many cat owners, it may seem that their feline is asleep more time than he is awake, and they are right. The hours spent in sleep vary from feline to feline, with most cats sleeping from 12 to 16 hours in any 24-hour period, and even up to 20 hours for young kittens and older cats.

The Importance of Sleep

Just as with people, sleep helps build muscles and bones in kittens and it provides natural regenerative healing for felines of any age. Unlike people, rare is the cat who suffers from insomnia. If your cat is up all night it's likely that it's not because he's a problem sleeper, but because he slept all day.

🐾 Cat Fact

As part of the Felidae family, our cats are related to lions, who are also known to sleep much of the time. As the primary hunter, the female lion may sleep for up to 20 hours per day.

Sleep, Little Kitten

Kittens are born in a more immature state than most mammals, and need even more sleep in the first month of their life than the generous amount of sleep they enjoy as adults. This works out well, since sleep provides a natural "baby-sitter" when their mother leaves the nest to get food. It keeps the kittens quiet and together, safely out of a predator's sight.

SLEEP STAGES

Although they spend substantially more time with their eyes closed, the sleep patterns of our felines are very like our own. When asleep they too start out in a light wave sleep, a non-dream stage of sleep. After about 30 minutes, they pass into a deeper REM sleep, characterized by rapid eye movement. During this period, your cat's body will appear deeply relaxed but his paws, ears, and mouth may twitch, indicating that cats—like people—dream during REM sleep, when their bodies rest but their minds are active. For the remainder of his sleep, he will cycle between short periods of deep sleep followed by light sleep, for a total of 20 to 30 percent of REM sleep. If your cat is taking a nap, rather than settling in for a longer sleep, he will not reach the REM stage of sleep. He remains in light wave sleep, easily roused and ready to spring into action if needed.

PREDATORY SLEEPING PATTERNS

The sleeping pattern of our felines is that of the hunter and predator. They sleep more than most mammals, and

🐾 Cat Fact

Cats are normally referred to as nocturnal. However, "crepuscular," the term used to describe animals who tend to be most active at dawn and dusk, would be a more accurate description for many felines.

this helps them to conserve energy that will be used in sudden and frenetic bursts of play and hunting. Stocking up on sleep in this way is possible due to their protein-rich diet. In the wild, herbivores sleep an average of one-third the amount the carnivorous cat does, and this is because grazing takes a significant amount of time, something the meat-eating cat who hunts in short bursts does not need to worry about. A look at the behavior of cats in the wild offers further explanations for the sleep patterns of our felines. As lone hunters, adult cats in the wild do not have a pack, in the way dogs do, to look out for them. Cat naps enable them to rest, yet be fully alert if a predator approaches. During this time the cat's senses are still active, keeping him in touch with his surroundings even while sleeping.

BEHIND THE SIGNS

Third Eyelid

The thin cover of the nictitating membrane, or third eyelid, of your cat allows light in when he naps. Any change in light patterns tells the dozing cat that something in his environment has changed, and he will be instantly alert to ensure it was not the shadow of a predator. However, if your cat has settled in for a deep sleep he may not be as easily roused and it is best not to startle cats awake. They may react fearfully, and use their claws in self-defense.

WHERE AND WHEN TO SLEEP

Cats have a wonderful ability to sleep anywhere, and favorite spots include a sunny window ledge, the bed that carries their owner's scent, the warm drum of the clothes dryer if a careless owner has left the door open, and in the shade of the garden. If their people are home during the day, many cats will stay close, choosing a warm spot on cold days and curling up to conserve body heat, and finding a cool corner where he can stretch out to encourage heat loss on warm days. Your cat's sleeping spots tend not to be as random as they may appear, and there is usually a pattern based on the time of day and the season. If another cat usurps his spot this can lead to territorial scent-marking—spraying, clawing, bunting—used to claim an area as his own and send other felines a message.

Given the choice, most cats would be up most of the night, and sleep through the day. This can be disruptive to owners and is not conducive to bonding with your cat, since it limits your time together. To help your cat to sleep when you do, make sure he has toys to keep him stimulated and prevent boredom sleeping during the day. A few play sessions with you each evening can also help tire him out in time for your bedtime, although he will likely still wake you before your alarm in the morning!

His nose may twitch, his ears may move, and if anything is out of the ordinary he will become fully alert immediately. Cats also have a third eyelid that facilitates this restful yet on guard behavior. Known as the nictitating membrane, it is visible in some cats when they are very contented or very sleepy, and in other felines it rarely shows. It lies underneath the outer eyelid and one of its many functions is to act as an internal light sensor alarm. If a shadow falls across the eyes of a dozing cat he will wake instantly, and be asleep minutes later if the shadow proves not to be dangerous. Our domestic felines inherited these sleeping patterns as part of the parcel of hunting genes passed down to them, which is why cats are generally most active during the night

⊛ Cat Fact

Cats sleep more than most animals, with the exception of the sloth, who sleeps for 80 percent of his life.

and at dawn and dusk—prime time for nocturnal hunters—with naps and periods of sustained rest outside of peak hunting time. The sleeping behavior of our cats is dictated, or has evolved from, the best times to hunt. Depending on their prey, wild cats will adjust their sleeping patterns accordingly. If mice are their primary prey, they will hunt at night and sleep during the day. If the cold-blooded lizard is their primary prey, they will change their routine to sleep at night and hunt during the day when the lizard is out being warmed by the sun.

When cats wake they may yawn as we do, but their yawn is not just a sleepy gesture—it is also a greeting. Then comes stretching, to shake off the cobwebs of sleep and restore flexibility to muscles that have been at rest. The next part of the ritual is generally grooming their coat with their tongue, on which they may spend a total of up to 50 percent of their waking hours.

⊛ Cat Fact

Our felines sleep more than they are awake, but their sleep is not one long period of rest as it generally is with humans. Instead, they will have frequent cat naps, punctuated by longer periods of sleep.

AGGRESSIVE BEHAVIOR

UNDERSTAND THE MESSAGE

> "Most cats do not approach humans recklessly.
> Much ceremony must be observed, and
> a number of diplomatic feelers put out,
> before establishing a state of truce."
> —Lloyd Alexander, author

Aggression toward people is a behavioral problem most commonly associated with our canines, but is not something our felines are immune to. It is less common, but remains a significant reason that cats are abandoned to shelters. It can take many forms, from hissing when approached to scratching or biting. Understanding the cause can help you better manage the behavior, and change it.

A cat that suddenly develops aggressive behavior may be motivated by a medical condition, so the first step in isolating the cause should be a visit to your veterinarian. If the aggression is not health-related then it will typically fall into one of the following categories: play aggression, defensive aggression, territorial aggression, or misdirected aggression.

PLAY AGGRESSION

Play aggression is the most common type of problem aggression, and this typically starts out innocently enough. Owners play roughly with their kitten, for example, wrestling, and the kitten appears to enjoy it—and is likely reminded of play with his littermates during these sessions. Everyone is happy, until the kitten gets bigger, at which time the play behavior that has been encouraged can suddenly become a problem. This is not a vicious cat; it has simply been "trained" into inappropriate behavior. To retrain the cat, start by always making sure play involves a toy, rather than the hands and feel of the owner. Play can still be interactive, but instead of rolling the cat around with your feet use a ball or pole toy to put distance between what the cat has been trained to think of as toys—his human's feet and hands—and redirect the play activity. Give a sharp "no" when the cat gets aggressive with a person, and ignore him totally for at least five minutes. This means no looking at him or any form of acknowledgment. This cat likes attention, which is why he reached out to bite your foot in play, just as he had been encouraged to through laughter and attention as a kitten. If ignored each and every time he acts in a way he shouldn't he will get the message, and stop the behavior that gets him no response. Everyone in the household must do this consistently. In this type of aggression the cat is just doing what he has always been encouraged to do. He can learn appropriate behavior, as long as the message is made clear.

Cat Fact

If you act like another cat and play roughly with your feline he's going to treat you like another cat, and play roughly in return.

KIDS AND CATS

Children are typically the victims of feline aggression—a situation that is usually avoidable if the child is taught the appropriate behavior to use around cats. With the best intentions, children may attempt to hug cats, wrestle with them in play, or constrain them, and receive a scratch or bite in return. The best way to avoid this is to teach the children empathy for the cat, explaining how he might misread or not be comfortable with their enthusiastic friendliness. In a cat's eyes, quick movements and loud noises, especially when coming from those larger in size than him, can feel threatening. Same goes for teasing, rough play, and any form of constraint. Interaction is fine, as long as it is gentle and not forced.

The Importance of the First Eight Weeks

Research indicates that the relationship a cat enjoys with its mother plays an important role in determining the nature of its personality. Kittens that spend the first eight weeks of their lives with their mothers are generally less aggressive. Play and correction from their mother and littermates during this period teaches them when they are playing too rough.

DEFENSIVE AGGRESSION

Defensive aggression may occur suddenly, for example, when petting your cat. Everything may seem fine, and then he will lash out. If you look carefully at the signs, however, you will notice body language that precedes these outbursts. Your cat may have enjoyed the petting for the first five or ten minutes, but then his ears may have moved to face forward or be folded so that the backs are clearly visible. His tail may twitch and he may stare at you with intensity. This is all his way of saying he has had enough, and is feeling constrained. Listen to his message and let him go. This type of aggression doesn't mean your cat doesn't like affection; it simply means he likes it for a certain amount of time and then his threshold is reached. Learn to read the signals your cat sends you and listen to them. You can also gradually increase his threshold for affection or anything else—for example, car rides—by slowly increasing the time spent and making it a positive experience. If you want him to spend more time on your lap then give him treats that encourage him to stay.

Hands and Feet

When hands and feet are used as toys, it is safe to assume that cats will treat them as such. Kittens that are allowed to clamp down on a human finger won't know that this action is no longer appropriate when they reach a certain size. This is particularly pertinent in households where young children and adult cats interact. The key lies in teaching cats from an early age that hands and feet are off limit from the start—a simple way to prevent unnecessary and potentially nasty injuries.

He will make the connection, and once his threshold is increased you won't need the treats each time. If, however, while doing this you see your cat's body language change from relaxed to aggressive then let him go without a reward. You don't want to send him a mixed message by rewarding aggressive body language, and continuing on once he is already feeling defensive will only aggravate the situation. Give him his space and try again next time.

TERRITORIAL OR MISDIRECTED AGGRESSION

Territorial aggression is triggered by a threat to what the cat perceives as his territory. This type of aggression may be common feline to feline, but is very rarely directed at humans. The object of the cat's anxiety being out of reach, for example, a squirrel he can see through the window, causes redirected aggression. This type of aggression is also not common. When it happens, the best way to stop the behavior is to remove the cause, in this case, by closing the drapes.

Cat Fact

Cat-to-people aggression is rare, and one explanation is this: cats don't like to take any chances with their food supply.

Socialization

At the root of aggressive feline behavior is often a sense of fear brought on by unfamiliar surroundings and faces. Such displays of unwanted aggression are avoidable simply by giving your cat the opportunity and time to accustomize themselves to the house and its occupants, and also to the things outside of the house to which they may be exposed. Cats that have been properly socialized to people, other pets, and different experiences are rarely aggressive, because they are less fearful.

DESTRUCTIVE BEHAVIOR

TRANSLATE YOUR CAT'S ACTIONS

" Even if you have just destroyed a Ming Vase, purr. Usually all will be forgiven."
—Lenny Rubenstein, author

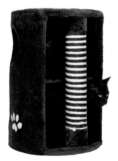

*D*estructive behavior is in the eye of the beholder. Your cat doesn't see the dining room table; he sees a message board. He doesn't see the banister, he sees an emery board. What seems destructive to you is natural behavior to your feline. He is not a problem cat when he claws at furniture and walls, he is just a cat. Scratching relieves his instinctive need to claw at objects to communicate his presence; and to play, exercise, and maintain his claws. But where your feline learns to scratch, his activity level and mental stimulation, and the amount of companionship he has are what will characterize his behavior as healthy or destructive.

Your cat comes from a long line of felines famous for their claws, who used them in the same ways. Lions, for example, also proclaim their territory by scent marking, and they sharpen their claws on trees. Unfortunately, destructive scratching is the behavior that causes the most frustration among cat owners. It is, however, an instinctive behavior, used not only for territorial marking (see Chapter 6), but also in play and for claw maintenance. It is one of those very feline behaviors that make a cat a cat; while you can't eradicate the behavior, you can redirect it by encouraging appropriate scratching that will keep both you and your cat happy.

⊛ Cat Fact

Prevention is better than a cure. If there isn't a scratching post provided your cat will create his own.

What Not to Do

Punishment is not the answer. Your cat will not make the connection between his scratching and the punishment; instead it will only serve to encourage him to be wary of you. Scratching is as instinctive as burying his droppings, so punishing him for the behavior will only confuse him. And, if your cat is scratching to mark territory, punishment will only increase his anxiety and insecurity.

DESTRUCTIVE CLAWING

WHAT YOU SEE:
Visible scratch marks on hard surfaces such as wallpaper, furniture, doors, and floors.

WHAT IT MEANS:
Your cat is not being vindictive or acting out. He doesn't know his behavior is inappropriate because to felines it is instinctive, and a very logical way to leave a message for other felines (see Chapter 6). It is also part of the natural wake-up routine for many felines. Stretching and scratching go together, and common is the sight of a waking cat stretching out against the floor and scratching against it as his body retracts and completes the stretch. Scratching is also part of a cat's play activity and part of his grooming, as it hones and cleans his claws.

WHAT TO KNOW:
If it has become a destructive behavior look for the cause. Is it territorial marking (see Chapter 6) or is it done in play or as part of your cat's grooming ritual? If it is either of the latter causes, a purpose-built scratching post can help redirect your cat's behavior away from your furniture. However, a scratching post only works if your cat is interested in it, so you may want to invest in one that comes imbedded with catnip, has multiple ledges for perching and climbing, is stable—wobbly posts are typically ignored by our felines, and—this is very important—is in a location in which your cat frequently scratches. Regular trimming of your cat's claws can also help limit damage, as can tacking double-sided adhesive sheets or aluminum foil against walls that your feline frequently visits with his claws. This provides an unpleasant sensation when scratched, at which time you can direct your feline to the approved scratching post. If using adhesive it should be about the strength of regular household tape so as not to cause damage to your cat's paws, and may need to be replaced daily to be effective, until your cat gets the message.

⊛ Cat Fact

The more cats you have the more scratching posts are needed. It is recommended that you have one additional scratching post per cat; therefore if you have one cat, two scratching posts should be sufficient.

To prevent boredom scratching, make sure your cat has toys that provide mental stimulation, along with lots of quality time with you.

Follow Your Feline's Example

Cats favor padded surfaces, like the sofa, and unvarnished wood, common to doors and furniture, for their destructive scratching. Choose similar materials for the scratching post and avoid hard, shiny surfaces, just as our felines do. Carpet is a favored material for scratching; although it might seem that using this material would encourage your cat to claw at other similarly covered areas in your home, this has not proven to be the case.

🐾 Cat Fact

The possible reasons for clawing behavior are many; the best way to translate your cat's actions is to look at the patterns of locations where the behavior occurs, and the dynamics of the home.

BEHIND THE SIGNS

Leave No Trace

Remove all signs of scratching from wooden furniture, doors, and banisters by sanding them and applying furniture polish so no trace remains. This is not for aesthetic reasons, but because the scratch marks are visible signals that encourage the cat to repeat the behavior in that location. A scratching post can instead be offered to the cat as an alternative. The siting of the post is critical to its successful use. It should be placed where your cat frequently spends his time, and close to any of the inappropriate places he may have clawed.

"CAT, MEET SCRATCHING POST"

To introduce your cat to a scratching post, place it in an area where your cat spends much of his time. If it is tucked away it won't be used. There are many commercial products available, or you can make your own with a four-by-four wood post. Use carpet tacks to adhere burlap sacks or carpet to it—a loop weave provides the appropriate degree of resistance. The post should be at the same height and incline as the furniture the cat likes to scratch, and should be placed nearby. Once the cat is using the post regularly it can gradually be moved to a more convenient location, moving it just a few steps away each day.

A fishing pole toy around the base of the post will encourage your cat to investigate, and once he has made contact with and scratched the post that behavior is likely to be repeated, particularly if you continue to encourage it with treats and praise. To encourage your cat to use a post with perches on different levels, place treats on the perches and let him explore. Remove all signs of his scratching in other locations, so that he has no visible reminders to trigger repeat behavior. Once your cat is using the post, you can introduce others in different locations. If they become ragged with use replace them at your own risk, as your cat may not accept the replacement.

TERRITORIAL MARKING

It's not always easy to tell the difference between territorial marking and the many other reasons your cat may choose to leave his mark. Generally, territorial marking is characterized by widespread scratching in different locations that are regularly targeted. It is also more common in homes where there has been recent upheaval, and in multi-cat households.

INAPPROPRIATE BEHAVIOR

SIGNIFICANCE AND SOLUTIONS

"The city of cats and the city of men exist one inside the other, but they are not the same city."
—Italo Calvino, author and journalist

So much of what we term "inappropriate" is natural behavior to cats, and they don't know it is wrong unless we teach them. Many people believe that cats can't be trained, but this is a myth. They may not be easily trained, but they are trainable. If they learn that an action doesn't get the response they want they will stop, as long as you send them the appropriate message consistently enough for them to understand it. If they learn that good behavior gets them treats and attention, they will repeat those behaviors.

Prevention is better than a cure, but when the undesirable behavior is already being exhibited then the best defense is to put a stop to the behavior, to prevent a problem that is frustrating from escalating into something more. For example, provide climbing posts or cat gyms to encourage your cat to jump up onto those, instead of your counter, tabletops, and stove. If the jumping up is already something your cat regularly does then you may need to get creative to stop the behavior: block off the area so your cat can't access it or use a water pistol to deter your cat when no other method works. If he associates jumping up on the stove with an unexpected squirting he will avoid that area, but this works best when he doesn't see where the water is coming from; it should be a surprise squirting he associates with the object he has jumped onto, and not with you.

1. COMPULSIVE GROOMING

WHAT YOU SEE:

Your cat engages in prolonged periods of self-grooming, which may result in loss of hair/bald patches on his coat or irritated skin.

WHAT IT MEANS:

It could be a medical condition, such as skin parasites, a fungal infection, or allergies. Or it could be psychological due to anxiety and stress.

WHAT TO KNOW:

All cats groom, but when extreme, like any behavior that goes beyond normal and generally harmless limits, it is a message that things are not right with your cat. If the behavior is new it could be due to a recent medical condition, such as skin parasites. Fleas can cause irritation that leads to over-grooming for relief. Skin infections are also a possibility due to fleas or mite infestations left untreated, or tangled and matted hair that can pull at skin and lead to hot spots. Look for round, raw lesions on the skin that are moist and inflamed. Hot spots may be the result of skin or coat problems, but they can also be caused when there is not a medical condition and be a direct result of the over-zealous licking behavior the cat gives to his hips or the sides of his chest, which itself causes irritation. Allergies are also a possibility. Non-medical causes are typically anxiety. Like humans, cats can engage in compulsive behaviors due to events they find traumatizing, and the threshold is different for each feline. What one cat may adapt to easily—such as a new addition to the home—can prove very stressful to another cat, particularly if they are highly strung or genetically predisposed to compulsive behaviors, as some breeds are. See your vet to rule out a medical condition and for advice on the best way to deal with the excessive grooming behavior of your cat, which may involve anti-anxiety medication.

> ## 🐾 Cat Fact
>
> *Hot spots may be the cause of the over-grooming or the result. Cats will lick, scratch, or bite at the inflamed and painful areas of their skin for relief, which results in further irritation.*

2. KNEADING

WHAT YOU SEE:
Your cat rhythmically pushes out and then against an object using his front paws in a kneading or paddling motion.

WHAT IT MEANS:
It is believed that when cats do this they are content, which is backed up by the fact that they often accompany the behavior with purring. This behavior may be directed to their owner's chest or, for example, the couch cushions. It typically precedes the cat settling down for a nap in a comfortable location.

WHAT TO KNOW:
Behaviorists theorize that this kneading is a remnant from early kittenhood, as it mimics the behavior used to help stimulate their mother's teat for feeding. Also known as paddling or treading, this behavior may be exhibited by any cat of any age, although it is more typical of the Siamese and Oriental breeds, who tend to be quite demonstrative cats. It is not behavior to worry about, although if it is directed at you it can be uncomfortable as the cat's claws are typically unsheathed at the time. Despite this there is nothing aggressive in this behavior. It is the sign of a relaxed and happy cat. Trimming your cat's claws regularly can help prevent kneading behavior that is directed at you from being painful. Cats typically knead their owner's chest from the comfort of their owner's lap; if the kneading becomes excessive, stand up to stop the behavior.

🐾 Cat Fact

Cats do not knead hard surfaces, but reserve this behavior for a soft and pliant surface.

3. EARLOBE SUCKING

WHAT YOU SEE:
Your cat may suck on a human's earlobe, or on parts of his own body.

WHAT IT MEANS:
A variant on wool sucking (see next page), this behavior mimics suckling and is comforting to the cats who do it.

WHAT TO KNOW:
Kittens should remain with their mother and littermates until they are eight weeks of age, but when this isn't possible the kitten that has been removed from the mother may suck at, for example, their own foreleg or, commonly, the earlobe of their owner. Their nursing may have been cut short if they were removed too early, which most often explains the behavior. In many cases they were not weaned or were weaned too early and, like wool sucking, earlobe sucking is a replacement behavior. Some owners don't mind the behavior but it can become disruptive, for example, when the cat wakes his owner up with the behavior. Prevention is the best cure, so if your cat is engaging in this behavior stand up and they will be forced to stop. Ignore your cat totally for five minutes or so—this includes not looking at your cat and no acknowledgment whatsoever. With consistency, cats that are not compulsive about earlobe sucking can learn that it is a behavior that does not get the results they intended, either comfort or attention. Chew toys should also be encouraged, and your veterinarian should be consulted if the problem persists or becomes excessive.

4. WOOL SUCKING

WHAT YOU SEE:
Your cat may suck on wool sweaters, blankets, and occasionally non-wool items as well.

WHAT IT MEANS:
It is believed to be a nervous, overly dependent trait, most often exhibited by cats who were weaned too early or are experiencing stress.

WHAT TO KNOW:
Some cats can be quite compulsive in their behavior, and some breeds are more prone to it, such as the Siamese and Burmese. This behavior is generally not worrisome in small doses, but can easily progress to a problem, particularly in cats who were abruptly weaned. Kittens with a strong drive to nurse who have been cut off early or abruptly typically suck wool as replacement nursing. Some outgrow it, just as they would progress from their mother's teat in the normal scheme of things. Others stop the behavior in general, but may revert to it occasionally. In worst-case scenarios, cats progress from sucking wool to eating it and other inappropriate objects, such as shower curtains and cushions. To prevent this behavior, ensure that clothing is put away and inaccessible. Try to remove the causes of stress in your cat's life, such as fighting between cats in multiple-cat households or anxiety from too much time spent alone. Attempt to redirect wool-sucking behavior by making chew toys available and encouraging their

use. The causes for wool-sucking behavior will not be the same for each cat, and depending on the reason and level of intensity there will be a different solution. The behavior may fade away, be seen only in times of upheaval and stress, or it may become compulsive. Occasional wool sucking in mildly affected cats is typically not problematic, but anything more is reason to speak to your veterinarian about the problem. In cases where the behavior is excessive, such as eating inappropriate objects, it can prove dangerous and life-threatening to your cat, so it needs to be addressed.

5. ARMPIT FIXATION

WHAT YOU SEE:
Your cat sniffs, and then vigorously rubs his face into your armpit. He may drool, and lick at or grip the area.

WHAT IT MEANS:
Your cat's world revolves around his sense of smell. There are glands in our armpits that release scent that may not be noticeable to us but our felines are attracted to it, just as they are to sleeping in the bed that carries our scent, or on the clothes we wore that day. The sense of taste is also strongly related to smell and cats are attracted to salt, a component of sweat found on skin.

WHAT TO KNOW:
Cats have a sense of smell approximately 14 times stronger than ours and are very attracted to the unique pheromones each human has. No matter how clean we may be, their very sensitive noses are still attuned to our scent, and because of the scent glands in our armpits this area is very attractive to them. Cats can become so excited when burrowing into an armpit that their reaction can be similar to that of a cat enjoying catnip. This isn't really a problem, although it is best to discourage this behavior as it can become more frequent if allowed. It can also become disruptive, and what may seem humorous at first may seem less so when you are woken up because of it. The best way to prevent this behavior is to stand up, and then ignore your cat for a few minutes. He can't reach your armpit when you are standing so the behavior is stopped and, since he doesn't like to be ignored, with consistency on your part he will stop repeating behaviors that don't get him the desired results.

6. EATING/DIGGING UP HOUSEPLANTS

WHAT YOU SEE:
You may see your cat in the act of eating or digging up houseplants, or you may only see the telltale sign that is the ravaged plant.

WHAT IT MEANS:
Like dogs, cats sometimes eat greenery to aid in their digestion or because they like the taste of it. To some cats, the soil or compost of plants provides the same function as litter.

WHAT TO KNOW:
It is not known whether the act of eating grass is the cat self-medicating and purposely eating the plant to induce vomiting, or if the carnivorous cat is simply attracted to the plant. Either way, the eating of houseplants can be dangerous because many are toxic to cats, for example, calla

🐾 *Cat Fact*

An occasional, isolated episode of vomiting is typically not something to worry about if your cat follows it up with normal behavior. Contact your veterinarian if the vomiting is persistent or frequent and/ or your cat seems lethargic or uninterested in food, as this indicates a more serious problem.

lily, chrysanthemum, daffodil, ivy, lily, mistletoe, philodendron, poinsettia, and more. Some felines may use the soil or compost of plants as an alternate litter, perhaps because their litter box is not fresh enough, or simply because the plant is there. To prevent the eating or digging up of plants, keep them safely out of reach, taking into account the fact that cats are great climbers and jumpers. Foil underneath the plant is also a deterrent to cats who don't like the feel of it on their paws. Mothballs in a cloth bag placed atop the soil can also help keep determined cats away, as most don't like the smell.

7. BRINGING HOME PREY

WHAT YOU SEE:
Small prey, alive or dead, that your cat has brought home.

WHAT IT MEANS:
Cats are hunters. Your cat may bring home "gifts" from the hunt to share with you, just as wild cats bring home food to the nest. Or they may recognize you as a member of their group without hunting skills, and bring prey home so you can hone your skills.

WHAT TO KNOW:
Punishment is ineffective. This is natural and inherited cat behavior, so any punishment will result in confusing your cat and may cause him to mistrust and avoid you. The best defense is prevention. Keep your cat in during his prime hunting time, which is usually at dusk and dawn. Placing bells on your cat's collar can help alert prey that he is nearby, and if the hunt is unsuccessful your feline won't be bringing anything back. If your cat is prone to this behavior, it's a good idea to remove any bird-feeding stations you may have in your garden or to hang them higher up, so as not to make the hunting too easy for him. Bird tables constructed above metal poles also make it more difficult for your cat to climb up, giving his prey more time to get away. Hunting is not related to diet or hunger; it is behavioral and intrinsic to felines.

PROBLEM BEHAVIOR

TRANSLATE THE BEHAVIOR TO DETERMINE THE SOLUTION

" Cats can be cooperative when something feels good, which, to a cat, is the way everything is supposed to feel as much of the time as possible."
—Roger Caras, photographer and author

Our cat's behaviors can sometimes be inexplicable to us, which only makes sense. They are a different species after all, who speak a different language. They can't tell us why they are refusing to use their litter box or turning up their nose at the new cat food you have given them. It's up to us to take a closer look at what's going on in our cat's world to understand what their behavior communicates, and make the changes that will translate problem behavior into desired behavior.

LITTER BOX AVOIDANCE

Cats may stop using their litter box for a number of wide-ranging reasons—and there is always a reason, however challenging it may be to figure out. To understand your cat's behavior, start by knowing that although he may be sending you a message, he is not acting out because he is mad at you. Cats instinctively bury their urine and feces so if your cat is not doing this he may be communicating a medical condition. Cats can suffer from urinary tract problems that can seriously impact their health. It is more common in males, because the tube that empties urine from their bladder, the urethra, is narrower than that in females and can become more easily plugged. This is painful, and can cause your cat to associate the pain of urination with his litter box. If your cat is not using his litter box or is straining to go, contact your veterinarian. A blockage can lead to a buildup of toxins, which can quickly be life-threatening or lead to organ damage. Your veterinarian can determine if this is the case, or if it is diabetes-related. Diabetes may translate as your cat having to urinate frequently, in which case he may not always make it to his litter box in time.

FASTIDIOUS FELINES

If the problem is not medically related, it could be due to the naturally fastidious nature of our cats. Their sense of smell is highly developed and can be up to 14 times stronger than ours, so what may smell perfectly fine to us may cause our cats to look for somewhere else to relieve themselves. If your cat has suddenly stopped using his box, give it a good cleaning with hot soapy water and then a coating of fresh litter. If he still refuses to use his box look to any recent environmental changes. Have you changed the location of the box? Your cat may not like the new location if it is too close to where he eats, if it is in a high-

What Not to Do

Regardless of how often your cat tests your patience by wilfully ignoring your commands and even behaving in a way that seems to you antagonistic, punishment is not the answer. It can increase problem behavior by making the cat more anxious, or through association—for example, being forcibly placed in a litter box after soiling on the floor—which can cause the cat to avoid the box because of the negative experience. If you want your cat to acquire desirable habits, then they must be associated with positive outcomes in his mind, which means your encouragement must be unfailing, no matter how frustrated you might feel!

⊛ *Cat Fact*

Kittens sometimes forget where their litter box is, particularly when they are very young. Place it away from their food bowls but still in sight, so they have a constant reminder of its location. Elderly cats may suffer from mobility problems, which can make getting to the litter box in time difficult.

traffic area or is too isolated, or if it has been placed next to a loud appliance or where there is a draft. Have you changed the box itself, or the type of litter? If your cat is used to an open box and is presented with one with a lid, this may be enough for him to go elsewhere. If the litter is scented or is clumping, is too hard or too soft, or there is not enough of it or too much of it in the box this can cause your cat to avoid it. Two common reasons that cats soil outside of their box include: 1) they feel threatened by another cat in the house, and 2) they associate their box with punishment. If you have a multi-cat household you should have multiple litter boxes in different areas to avoid territorial squabbling and anxiety, which can lead to soiling or spraying in the home to mark territory (see Chapter 9). If your cat has soiled outside his box in what was an isolated incident and been punished for it by forcibly being placed in his litter box, that experience may cause him to avoid it.

Figuring out why your cat is acting as he is may take some trial and error, but there is a message in his behavior. Too many cats are abandoned because they soil in the house, but generally this is a problem that has a solution. Experiment with a new litter and box if need be, or return to what was previously used with success. If your cat has developed a preference for eliminating on clothing or carpet it may

be because he prefers the soft surface. In this case, try using shredded newspaper or wood shaving in the box, or even a piece of carpet, frequently changed, as a last resort. In the latter case if your cat responds well to the carpet you can slowly add a soft litter on top of it, increasing the amount every couple of days to help him get used to it until you are able to remove the carpet from his box. Cats that eliminate easily outside while avoiding a litter box may respond to soil in their box. Cats who eliminate on tile or wood flooring may prefer an empty litter box, or one with litter only on one side so they can eliminate on a hard surface yet still cover their urine and feces, as is generally their instinct. Ensure that what you interpret as soiling is indeed that, and not spraying behavior, which has different causes and solutions (see Chapter 9). If your cat has gotten into the habit of avoiding his litter box, for whatever reason, you may need to entice him back. Put a secondary litter box in the area that he is using to relieve himself to see if that will encourage him to use the litter instead of the floor. Or put his food and water bowls in the inappropriate area where he is eliminating, as cats do not like to eliminate where they eat and drink. Aluminum foil on the floor can also be a deterrent as most cats dislike the feel of it, and will avoid venturing into an area where it is placed. Clean any inappropriate elimination areas thoroughly

are training their cat to be a problem eater. Cats do not get bored with their food, unless they figure out that being picky is self-rewarding, because their owners scramble to provide something else. In this case, the best way to deal with the problem is to give your cat food that he has eaten in the past. If he ignores it, then remove it after 30 minutes, and don't put any other food down until the next scheduled feeding. Hold off on treats during this time as well. At the next feeding, put down fresh food, once again removing it after 30 minutes if your cat does not eat. A hungry cat will eat the food placed before him, and learn that finicky behavior doesn't pay off. This may take a few days, but is generally successful.

so that any lingering smell does not trigger repeat offenses. This may involve using a fluorescent black light that will display urine stains not otherwise visible, and cleaning with products specially formulated to remove urine and feces odors that may be detectable to our cats, even when they aren't to us.

FINICKY FELINES

Cats are often reputed to be picky about their food when the reality is this is usually learned behavior. As long as you are feeding your cat a high-quality and nutritionally complete food they are generally content to eat the same meal daily, unless they learn otherwise. Owners that vary their cat's diet frequently and rush to respond when the cat doesn't immediately take to a certain flavor

If, on the other hand, your cat is not being finicky but has suddenly gone off his food and continues so for subsequent feedings there may be two possibilities: 1) his food is placed too close to where he eliminates, in which case changing the location of food bowls can change his behavior; or 2) he is ill. Sudden changes in eating behavior can signal a medical condition, particularly if accompanied by lethargy or any behavior that is unusual.

If you do need to change the food you normally feed your cat, do so gradually over three or four days. Give your

Cat Fact

Cats can most easily distinguish between salty, bitter, and sour, and avoid sweet-tasting foods.

cat a portion of the food he normally eats, with approximately a quarter serving of the new food, increasing the amount of the new food in small increments daily while weaning him off the food he is accustomed to. Cats are creatures of routine, and any sudden change can lead to problem feeding.

The Nose Knows

As is the case with many other animals, including humans, a cat's sense of taste is closely related to scent. This knowledge can help you encourage your cat to eat, particularly if he has been acting indifferently toward food. Try feeding him food that is at room temperature rather than directly from the fridge; the colder the food is, the less scent it gives, which means it is certainly going to seem less appealing to your fussy cat.

A GUIDE TO UNDERSTANDING COMMON QUESTIONS

"The really great thing about cats is their endless variety. One can pick a cat to fit almost any kind of decor, color, scheme, income, personality, mood. But under the fur, whatever color it may be, there still lies, essentially unchanged, one of the world's free souls."

—Eric Gurney, cartoonist and illustrator

*C*ats can be maddeningly aloof, entertaining, affectionate, and, at times, quite incomprehensible. Why do they keep such early morning hours, and insist you be awake as well? What explains the frenetic activity bursts they sometimes have in the evening, and is it really the result of a cat's sixth sense? Why are cats said to have nine lives, and is it true that they always land on their feet? Following is a guide to the most frequently asked feline questions. You don't need to know the answers to love your cat. You already do, even if you can't understand why he behaves as he does, but with insight into his behavior your bond is strengthened.

WHY DO CATS BURY THEIR WASTE?

Kittons are born with the instinct to cover their waste. Cats in the wild do it, even though they don't learn it from their mothers, since she does it away from the nest. Although the behavior is instinctive, it serves a valuable purpose in the wild, as it reduces odors that could alert predators to the presence of the cat.

Cats communicate through scent. When waste is not buried, it is generally a territorial message to other felines. This occurs in the wild, where the dominant cat may leave his feces uncovered while the subordinate cat covers his. In domestic cats, this behavior is sometimes seen in multi-cat households where there may be dominance and territorial issues between the felines. The cat that does not cover his feces is communicating through the scent of his waste that it is his territory. Cats that are anxious or stressed due to challenges from other cats or upheaval may leave their waste uncovered as well, as its scent is reassuring and confidence-boosting.

WHY ARE CATS SO ALOOF?

Cats have this reputation, but many cat owners wouldn't agree that cats are aloof. They show their affection differently than we do, and differently than dogs—who they are so often compared to—do. Cats are subtle. No madly wagging tail and jumping up and down, but generally a purr and a tail held aloft as they walk forward in greeting. Cats come from a long line of solitary hunters. They did not work as a group to hunt, but traveled alone. This means that for many cats it is ingrained in them to be more wary about the alliances they make. They are willing to meet a human halfway, but only once that human has proven they can be trusted. Until you understand their language, many cats may give off the impression of aloofness, but there are also breeds like the Sphynx, American Shorthair, and the Devon Rex, among others, who are visibly social, following their owners around and needing, emotionally, to be part of everything they do.

Cats can suffer from separation anxiety just as canines do, although it is less common. This may be because cats are not pack animals and, although they can be very social, they are often quite independent. However, overly needy cats, particularly those that have been removed from their mother and littermates too early, may show distress when their owner leaves for the day. This behavior is often accompanied by increased vocalization when alone, and perhaps vomiting or litter box avoidance. Key in identifying this as separation anxiety is that the problem behavior is only exhibited when the cat is alone, and not when the owner is home. The cat may also be over-enthusiastic when greeting their owner on their return. To treat and lessen this behavior, make goodbyes less difficult by ignoring your cat totally for at least 15 minutes before you leave home. Reassuring the cat and soothing him may only increase his anxiety, as your behavior confirms to him that he does indeed have something to worry about. Leave a toy or two out that is only available to your cat when you are not home, to keep him physically and mentally stimulated while you are out, and so he associates alone time with positive experiences. In the wild, cats hunt for food and all cats carry the hunting instinct, so the toys that will keep him most occupied may be "work-for-food" toys, where he has to puzzle out the treat. When you arrive home, ignore any frantic greeting, only paying attention to your cat once he has calmed down, at which time you should reward his behavior with some interactive play. Be patient and consistent with your cat; never acknowledge problem behavior but reward desired behavior, and you will soon have a well-behaved feline, and one that can happily spend time alone.

WHAT MAKES FELINES APPEAR SO GRACEFUL?

Cats are digitigrades—they walk on their toes, which facilitates quick take-offs when sprinting after prey, and as they walk they place each hind paw almost exactly where the corresponding forepaw was. This leaves minimal tracks and provides traction when hunting, but it also gives felines a "catwalk" gait, similar to that of models on a runway. Their way of walking appears very precise, and although a cat's gait is similar to other mammals when trotting—two back legs moving simultaneously alternating with two simultaneous front legs—they also use a diagonal gait when walking: two legs on one side of their body move first, before the legs on the other side of their body. Cats have a superior sense of balance, due to the vestibular apparatus located in their inner ear and the caudal vertebrae in their tails that contribute to balance. When sprinting quickly around corners their tail acts as a counterbalance, keeping them grounded even when their paws don't appear to touch the ground and contributing to their dancer-like grace.

WHY ARE CATS SAID TO HAVE "NINE LIVES"?

This myth is likely based on:

- Cat worship in ancient Egypt. The Egyptians believed that cats had close ties to their gods and deities, including Atum-Ra, who took the form of a cat on visits to the underworld and was said to have nine lives.
- The ability of cats to escape from dangerous situations. The senses of a cat are highly developed and their keen eyesight, sensitive hearing, and sense of smell alert them to danger early. Their agility and sense of balance helps them land on their feet and survive falls from high places, although, contrary to another myth, cats do not always land on their feet.

WHY DON'T CATS LIKE SWEETS?

Cats can distinguish between salty, bitter, sour, and sweet, and prefer the first three. They have trouble with sweet-flavored foods because they lack the gene to properly taste them. Most cats will avoid sweet flavors, with those that ingest sweet food often suffering indigestion later. Cats are carnivorous, and their mostly meat diet is well suited to them.

WHY DO CATS SNIFF BUTTS?

Just as dogs do with other dogs, cats do this to say hello and learn something about the other feline. Cats communicate through scent, and the scent glands around the anus can tell them much about the other cat, including sexual status.

DO CATS UNDERSTAND TIME?

It may seem that they do, as they are creatures of habit who like their dinner to be served at the same time each day, and they seem to be able to sense half an hour before an alarm clock will go off and so typically wake their owners then. Experts have shown that cats can understand what is known as "fixed-interval responses." In tests, cats given a job to do, such as pressing a lever, have figured out just when to do it to get the scheduled reward, and wait until then to perform.

WHY DO CATS DISLIKE CAR RIDES?

Not all cats dislike car rides, but many do. Cats are generally homebodies who like to stay close to their territory and range. They also don't generally like to be constrained, as they are in a car. Some cats get carsick, and car rides can be noisy and smelly. With their keen sense of hearing and smell, the sound of the automobile is much louder to them, and any smells are much stronger. Lastly, cats may associate car rides with bad experiences as it is the car that takes them to the veterinarian and it was the car that took them away from their mother and littermates.

DO CATS ALWAYS LAND ON THEIR FEET?

Yes—whenever they don't land on another body part, that is. The myth that cats always land on their feet may be rooted in the cat's noted sense of balance, but they do not always land on their feet. The vestibular apparatus located in their inner ear tells them which way is up and when they fall they are often able to rotate their very flexible bodies to lessen the impact and land feet up much of the time, but not every time. In AD 962, legend has it that cats were thrown from a tower in Belgium. Their ability to walk away amazed the townspeople and the spectacle has since been recreated annually, but with toy cats as of 1817.

Cat Fact

The term "High-Rise Syndrome" (HRS) is used to describe the traumatic injuries a cat may suffer from a fall from an apartment balcony or window.

WHY DO CATS COUGH UP HAIRBALLS?

Up to 50 percent of a cat's waking hours are spent in grooming. During this time your cat licks his coat clean, ingesting hair along the way. When too much hair collects in the stomach it can irritate the stomach lining and be coughed back up, instead of passing through the gut. It is a common problem, and one that longhaired cats may suffer from more often. Occasional hairball episodes of up to approximately four per month are generally nothing to worry about, but if it is more frequent it's best to have your cat checked by your veterinarian. Daily brushing can help prevent hairballs, by getting rid of the loose hair that might otherwise be ingested.

Do Hairless Cats Have Whiskers?

Some do and some don't. Cats described as hairless may sometimes have a very short, downy coat that sheds and does not regrow, as in the Sphynx, and some may have fur on their ears, muzzle, tail, and/or feet. They may have whiskers like other cats, they may have abnormal whiskers, or they may have no whiskers at all.

WHY DO CATS CHASE THEIR TAILS?

Occasional tail chasing may be done out of boredom or as a way to release aggression or anxiety, but if it is a new and repetitive behavior or frequent and intense it can communicate a medical or behavioral problem. If this is a new behavior there may be something irritating your feline in his tail region, such as anal gland problems or fleas. If the behavior is frequent and intensely focused it may be a behavior problem, such as an obsessive compulsive behavior that has been triggered because of genetics or environment. Either way, see your veterinarian. Tail chasing may seem cute and amusing, but it is generally a message that something is wrong.

WHY DOES MY CAT WAKE ME UP AT DAWN EVERY MORNING?

Cats are crepuscular, so are most active at dawn and dusk. Cats come from a long line of hunters whose prey is most active at this time, so their sleeping patterns evolved to follow suit. Key in changing this behavior is not paying any attention to the cat in the early-morning hours. Shut your bedroom door and ignore him even if you can hear him meowing and pawing at your door. Feed him at regularly scheduled times, and not too early in the morning. If you do this consistently, your cat will understand that there is nothing to be gained—neither food nor attention—in the early morning hours, but you must be consistent. If you give in even occasionally you are teaching your cat that his early-morning antics work, and he will continue. Make sure he has toys to keep him busy, and don't allow him to set the morning routine.

BEHIND THE SIGNS

Always Aware

Owners are often amazed at how their apparently soundly sleeping cat is up immediately when he hears the sound of dinner. This is because when your cat is napping his senses are still active and keep him in touch with his surroundings. Cats also have an inherited ability to be alert immediately if something in their environment needs to be investigated, and that most definitely includes dinner.

WHY AND HOW DO CATS ARCH THEIR BACKS SO DRAMATICALLY?

Cats do this as a defensive reaction, to make themselves look as intimidating as possible when threatened. It's a common reaction in animals. Dogs will make themselves look as big as possible to send an intimidating message, as will the cobra snake when it raises the front part of its body and spreads its neck. Cats are able to do this because of their flexible spines, which contain twice as many vertebrae as humans have. This action will typically be accompanied by the cat's hair standing on end, known as piloerection, which also contributes to him looking larger and more fearful. This body language sends the message "don't mess with me," and although it is usually fear-based, cats will act out with aggression if they feel the need to protect themselves.

Cat Fact

Cats have 13 thoracic vertebrae and seven lumbar vertebrae, which facilitate enhanced spinal flexibility. In comparison, humans have 12 and five respectively.

THE CAT CRAZIES

Your normally sedate cat may suddenly start racing around the room, darting quickly here and there while meowing frequently. What is it he sees and what has set him off? Some describe this behavior as the result of a cat's sixth sense, while others explain it as due to the highly developed smell, hearing, and vision a cat has. They may indeed sense something that we can't. Or, and this is frequently the reason for the behavior in kittens, your cat may suddenly have a burst of energy and feel the need to run it off. This behavior is more frequent, or perhaps just more noticeable, in indoor cats. All cats are predators, built for short bouts of frenetic hunting activity. When they don't have this, they may exhibit excited, energetic behavior for a short time indoors and particularly in the evening, when their hunting instinct is strong. It is usually nothing to worry about, although the behavior could be caused by a health condition, so it is always best to consult your veterinarian. Your cat may be racing around to relieve irritation from fleas, or he may be experiencing Feline Hyperesthesia Syndrome (FHS), a more serious condition, characterized by the skin on his back appearing to ripple. Sometimes called "twitchy cat disease," a cat suffering from FHS may exhibit strange behaviors and vocalizations, usually triggered by being touched. He may run and jump and even seem to hallucinate, and is usually very focused and intense during this time.

WHAT YOUR CAT'S HEALTH COMMUNICATES

"Cats are intended to teach us that not everything in nature has a purpose."
—Italo Calvino, author and journalist

C ats communicate with us through their body language, vocalization, and behaviors, but their health also has a message. To interpret it, monitor your cat's health and any behavior that is not normal for him. It's how your cat tells you if something is wrong, and when we understand our cat's language we can catch health problems early and take the appropriate steps to respond to our feline.

A healthy cat is an alert and curious cat. He grooms himself regularly, his appetite is good, as are his litter box habits. Home health checks, as part of grooming, can also help you note any changes that may signal ill health, while providing an opportunity to bond with your feline. While grooming, check that you can feel your cat's ribs. Visible ribs translate to an underweight cat, but if you can't feel his ribs he is generally overweight. A healthy cat has an hourglass shape with a noticeable waist. Next look at your cat's skin and coat. Skin should be smooth, with no scaly areas or red patches, which could indicate allergies, parasites, or infections. Your cat spends up to 50 percent of his waking hours grooming, and his coat should show it. Healthy coats are shiny and smooth, while dull and brittle coats can signal nutritional deficiencies. Shedding is normal, but excessive shedding and bald patches are not and, like skin problems, may signal parasites, such as fleas; irritations, such as hot spots; or may be an allergic reaction. Discharge from the ears can also signal parasites. Ears should be pink inside with no strong-smelling odor. Eyes should be clear and your cat's third eyelid should not be visible, as that is often a sign of stress and ill health. Gums should be pink, and teeth should have no buildup. Your cat's mouth doesn't need to be sweet-smelling to be healthy, but foul breath is indicative of a problem.

When you clean the litter box, note any changes in your cat's waste. Strong-smelling urine or watery stools are not healthy. Stools should be small and firm, a sign of good nutrition and digestion.

You know your cat best. What may be normal for one cat can indicate a problem in another; the key is in noting any changes and what they can tell you about your cat's health.

COMMON HEALTH CONCERNS

Cat Flu: Cats experiencing the flu are generally miserable, and it can be a dangerous condition in very young or older cats. Symptoms are varied but include runny nose and eyes, loss of appetite, mouth ulcers, and joint pain.

Ear Infections: The most common cause of ear infection is ear mites, a parasite that thrives in the warm moist area of the ear. Waxy discharge, head shaking, and scratching are common symptoms, and your cat may recoil from being touched around his head.

Fleas: The most common feline skin allergy is to fleas, which can cause constant scratching and biting at his body. It is easily treatable and many cats, especially if they are outdoor/indoor cats or come into contact with other animals, experience fleas at some point.

WARNING SIGNS

If your cat suddenly resists handling or shows aggression, this typically signals pain, as does hiding for prolonged periods or changes in appetite or litter box habits. Frequent vomiting, increased or decreased thirst, and loss of appetite are all messages to heed.

If your cat's stool is watery, if he is urinating excessively, straining to urinate, or avoiding his litter box there is a definite problem. A dull coat and eye appearance, listless behavior, or excessive chewing at skin, hair, or body parts all translate to something being wrong.

Hairballs: A common cat problem, it is only worrisome if it is frequent, as it can lead to dehydration and stomach ailments. If your cat is coughing up hairballs more than four times a month it could be a problem.

Vomiting: If your cat vomits but acts alert and remains interested in food it is generally not something to worry about. Occasional vomiting is normal, due to hairballs or eating too quickly. Frequent and prolonged vomiting, however, can be serious and requires a veterinarian checkup.

Worms: Hookworm, roundworm, and tapeworm are all common ailments that can be treated with medication. If infected, your cat's belly may expand, although he will generally lose weight overall, his coat may appear dull, and he may experience frequent vomiting.

BEHIND THE SIGNS

What Does It All Mean?

Many symptoms may be shared between conditions, so your veterinarian is the best person to translate them by providing a diagnosis. Itching and chewing of skin could mean fleas, which are common and easily treatable, or it could signal something more serious, such as skin cancer. A cat's sleeping habits can also indicate underlying health issues; if he is sick he will often not curl up to sleep but will instead lie in the position requiring the least energy.

⊛ Cat Fact

Any new behaviors, like excessive head shaking, can signal a problem. In this case it is likely parasites, but a thorough checkup is necessary to know for sure.

SLEEP, GROOM, EAT, AND PLAY

INSIGHT INTO A TYPICAL DAY

"Dogs have owners, cats have staff."
—Anonymous

Whoever said it's a dog's life hasn't spent much time with cats. Sleeping and grooming take up most of the cat's day, with routine daily tasks like eating and play taking up the remainder. Cats are skilled sleepers, and can spend up to 16 hours a day asleep. That may leave approximately eight hours awake, of which up to four hours may be spent in grooming.

Sleeping is a supremely feline trait. Although all animals do it, none but the sloth partakes as much as our felines. Individual and environmental factors will determine just how much your cat sleeps, but it is safe to say it is a lot, and that sleep will be the activity at which he spends the most time. Your cat may make himself comfortable in the corner of the couch by the window, kneading the cushions first to indicate he is settling in for a sleep. During sleep his ears, nose, and whiskers may move, because even in rest his senses are working to tell him what is going on around him. He may jump up a few times during sleep, to investigate the shadow or a noise from outside the window, but he then returns to sleep quickly. When he wakes from one of the many naps he will take that day, he works the muscles that were at rest, stretches to regain flexibility, and then will begin his grooming ritual, licking his coat clean to keep it shiny and pliant.

Cat Fact

Cats like routine. Try to feed your feline at the same times each day and spend at least 15 minutes with him twice a day, grooming or playing with him.

Cats will use their litter boxes throughout the day; frequency of visits will depend on the individual physiology of the cat and how much and what kind of food the cat is eating. At various points in the day your cat will visit his food and water bowls. The number and size of meals depends on your cat's age, health, and preference. Key is finding what works for you and your cat and sticking to it. Too much food leads to an overweight cat and health problems. Too little food will make it difficult for your cat to maintain good health. Growing kittens are usually fed more frequently than adult cats are; they typically receive up to three meals a day, which changes to one or two meals from age six months and up.

A few times a day, generally after grooming and eating, your cat will patrol his territory—the area where he sleeps and spends most of his time—and/or his range, a larger area than his territory and generally the area he inhabits, including the yard or garden if he has access to the outside.

The Grooming Ritual

Grooming is learned as a kitten by watching their mother. Cats typically follow her example and grooming practices may vary from feline to feline, but it generally takes place upon waking from sleep. Most start their grooming ritual with their faces, licking their mouth, chin, and whiskers. Your cat may scrub his face and around his head with a dampened front paw, before moving on to his shoulders, legs, flanks, genitals, and then his tail. He will typically switch to a rear paw to groom his neck and ears, and will scratch at and claw objects for claw maintenance.

🐾 Cat Fact

Cats conserve energy while asleep, to be used in short bouts of energetic hunting play.

If he feels it necessary, due to other felines in the home or neighborhood, he will back up against a vertical object or wall to spray and may claw at the fence or trees, scent-marking to announce his presence. After all of this activity it may be time for another nap, followed by more of the same along with some playtime. He may climb his cat gym or climbing post to survey his area, play with his fishing line and food-for-work puzzle toys, and practice his hunting skills with games of chase. Lastly, he may spend some time just staring: at his kingdom and the world around him or out the window, particularly if there is a bird feeder for him to watch.

INSIDE A CAT'S WORLD

A recent study by a leading cat brand manufacturer fitted 50 cats with cameras, in order to see what they did all day while their owners were away. While not conclusive, the study's findings are an interesting insight into our cat's world, and how our felines pass their time. Behavior scientist Dr. Jill Villarreal found the cats included in the study generally spent eight to 16 hours per day asleep, 12 percent of their day with any other animals in the home, five percent playing with toys, and more than 21 percent staring out the window. The study showed that when awake the cats were very active and, surprisingly, that in homes where there were other pets—and not just felines— the cats sought out their company.

No. 18 CAT SMARTS

FELINE INSTINCT AND INTELLIGENCE

" I have studied many philosophers and many cats. The wisdom of cats is infinitely superior."
—Hippolyte Taine, critic and historian

Cats have survived thousands of years in different environments, from the inquisition in medieval Europe to travel around the globe, and have shown themselves clever and adaptable. As lone hunters, cats in the wild are responsible for themselves. They are naturally self-reliant because they do not hunt and live with a pack, so survival is up to them alone. Our domestic cats may not have the same responsibilities as cats in the wild, but they have inherited those same smarts that have helped cats to survive for so long, in so many different conditions.

THE INTELLIGENT HUNTER

The predator instinct dictates much of our cats' behavior. They have evolved to hunt when their prey does, and adapted to humans because it was in human settlements that prey was more plentiful. Cats understand the concepts of availability and scarcity, and their scent-marking behavior and need for a defined territory and range show that they are able to connect the dots and understand cause and effect, and the logic of their lone hunter behavior.

TRAINABLE FELINES

The cat's brain is similar to a human brain, and has short-term and long-term memory. Cats learn through keen observation, first through watching their mothers and then through watching us as we go about our day. Observing their mothers teaches them the grooming habits so important to feline health, and observing us helps them to make connections and understand the world around them. For example, a cat who associates the sounds of dinner preparation with being fed will run happily into the kitchen whenever he hears the familiar sounds. He has made a connection between the rustling bag or the can opener through daily observation. Cats learn from trying out new behaviors to see what works, and once they have figured it out their keen memory means that they will typically never forget it. Cats that have been burned jumping up onto the stovetop

rarely jump up there again, and cats that have one bad experience with a canine will generally avoid all canines in the future. A cat that is introduced to a litter box typically has no need to be shown it twice. He will know what the litter box is for the next time he needs it and will seek it out from then on. Cats go to extraordinary lengths to solve problems. They will try different strategies, rejecting those that don't work and building on those that get them closer to their goals, as evidenced in their hunting methods—a definite sign of feline intelligence.

Cat Fact

Cats are known for their curiosity, and curiosity has long been recognized as intrinsic to intelligence.

We tend to look at cat intelligence through our human standards, which are subjective and generally anthropomorphic, interpreting a cat's behavior not through the eyes of a feline, but as if the cat was a human. Or, cats are very often compared to canines, and their different responses and ways of relating to their human family are interpreted negatively or positively depending on which side of the cat/dog debate resonates most with the individual. Cats are trainable, although many felines—smartly, some would say—are not interested in being trained. Dogs want to please us and are dependent on the approval of others. As pack animals, they are geared toward working for the betterment of the group. Cats, on the other hand, have no need to please anyone but themselves. As inherently solitary animals, their instinct is to do what is best for them, and not a group. This reality can sometimes make dogs appear smarter, as they seem to understand what is expected of them more readily, when the reality is that cats don't care what is expected of them, and as independent creatures don't need validation from others. That is not lack of brainpower, it is simply independence. The cat understands what behavior is desired, but chooses when to comply, if at all. As cat owners like to point out, you can't train a cat to pull a sled as you can a dog, so in the end who is smarter? The easily trainable canine now pulling a sled or the cat who ignored all attempts at training and is now blissfully grooming himself in a patch of sunlight?

Training Smarts?

Many dog owners point to the fact that canines are easily trainable as a sign of their superior intelligence. Cat owners, on the other hand, will counter that responding to commands and performing tricks doesn't equal smarts and point out that the cat keeps his own counsel, rather than have his behavior be dictated by others.

🐾 Cat Fact

Intelligence is often defined as an ability to problem-solve, a trait our felines have proven over and over, as any cat owner who has witnessed the Houdini-like antics of a cat to get into a locked cupboard can attest.

No. 19 FUN AND GAMES

MENTAL AND PHYSICAL STIMULATION THROUGH PLAY

"Anything not nailed down is a cat toy."
—Anonymous

Play is important for every cat. It can ease the stress of a new situation, help your cat release excess energy, build confidence, and can help multiple cats living in the same house to get along. Adult felines play for entertainment, stimulation, and exercise. Kittens play to improve their coordination and hone skills, particularly their experience as a hunter—a skill today's domestic cat may not need for survival, but one that is instinctively practiced through games regardless. All cats play for fun.

🐾 Cat Fact

Sprinkle some catnip on your cat's favorite toy and let him at it. Most cats will be deliriously pleased, and you'll be entertained watching him.

Play keeps cats mentally stimulated, lessening the chances of boredom-related behavioral problems. It's a positive way for your cat to release energy, and can improve many of the behaviors that frustrate cat owners. Nighttime wake-up calls can be prevented with a hearty play session in the evening, and cats that have toys available and are encouraged to play may stop looking at your feet and hands as playthings.

All cats have a highly developed prey and play drive, which translates to the most popular feline games being ones that involve stalking, chasing, swatting, and pouncing. The best games involve you and should take place at least twice a day, in sessions that are a minimum of 15 minutes. Most cat games are predatory in nature and success rate is important for successful play. A cat that is consistently unsuccessful in the hunt will lose interest,

just as one that catches his prey every time will become bored. Change it up for your cat, making him work for success, but letting him catch his prey every couple of games. Cats need no invitation to play independently, but interactive play with you improves the communication between you and your feline. It leads to a happier cat and gives you further insight into the secret language of felines, which translates to a stronger bond.

WHAT MAKES A GOOD TOY?

Just as cats don't need an invitation to play, they also don't need numerous store-bought toys. Household items that are cat-safe and can keep felines happily playing on their own for hours include the plastic tops from milk or juice containers, waxed paper balls rolled up tightly, large cardboard boxes, and—always a favorite—cardboard toilet-paper tubes.

Toys that are safe are ones that are not easy to swallow, so string and yarn—so often pictured with cats—are best kept out of reach. It is too often swallowed and this can cause a blockage of the intestinal tract followed by perforation, which would need immediate veterinary assistance and/or surgery. Plastic bags are another danger, so be especially careful to keep these in an area that your cat can't access.

Pet supply stores carry a wide assortment of popular cat toys, such as balls with bells, wand/fishing pole toys, and catnip-stuffed toys. Scratching posts can keep your cat happily occupied through jumping and climbing, while also helping to protect your furniture from scratches.

Keep Them Coming Back For More

Don't leave all of the toys out all of the time. It's a good idea to leave a few out for independent play, but the toys can become boring—and no challenge for your feline hunter—if they are always available. Praise your cat when he is successful, but save treats for the end of playtime. In the wild, eating takes place at the end of the hunt, so incorporating treats into the game can effectively tell your cat that the play session, or hunt, is over.

FUN AND GAMES

You help a cat's game come alive. Great games to play with your cat get him moving and incorporate hunting skills, just as all good cat games should.

Fishing

This is a classic game, enjoyed by felines and their people for countless years. Using a stick with a string and a feather, pretend to fish just over your cat's head. Move the feather back and forth and up and down so that your cat leaps after it. Allow him to catch the feather occasionally, but make the win a challenge.

Time to Play

Play is most successful when a cat initiates it. He may not be able to say the words "let's play," but when you see him racing around your home or hopping sideways this is exactly what he is telling you. To encourage your cat to play if he does not initiate it you may want to dim the lights, as cats prefer to "hunt" in dim light.

Peek-a-boo

Use a paper bag or an old towel and poke a few holes through it. Hold it up vertically and put a long straw or pipe cleaner through the hole, wiggling it around and drawing it in and out as your cat leaps and jumps after it. Vary the movement and the holes used to keep your cat motivated.

Chase

Move a fishing-pole toy or a string with a feather attached along the floor until your cat eyes it, and starts to stalk. As he follows it, move from room to room, keeping a few steps ahead of your cat and moving the string jaggedly to keep his interest. Let him pounce on the feather a few times, and then continue. This is great exercise for your cat, and a perfect way to release the energy he has stored up in frequent daytime naps.

Hide and Seek

Your cat may run across the room in front of you and then duck into a closet or under your bed, sneaking out to peek at you from his "hiding" spot. Run after him and he will race to his next hiding spot, and then the next.

Hunter/Predator

Use one of your cat's toys, for example, his squeaky mouse toy. Pretend the toy is being hunted by the cat, and roll it along the ground in "escape." Let your cat follow it and ambush it, not making it too easy, but letting him win occasionally and then giving him lots of praise.

Flashlight Tag

Turn off the room lights and turn on a flashlight or laser, pointing it at the wall so that the light appears on the wall's surface. Move the light around as your cat races across the floor and jumps up at the walls after it. Give your cat ample opportunity to work off some energy chasing the light and slow it down occasionally, letting him "catch" it before moving it again. This game is hugely entertaining to most felines, particularly if they don't connect you with the light, so do your best to move it around secretly.

Cat Fact

Toys to avoid include anything that your cat could easily swallow.

Ping-Pong

Rare is the cat who does not enjoy a good game of ping-pong. As you bounce the ping-pong ball on the floor or against a wall, your cat will actively take part in the game—jumping, pouncing, and swiping at the ball in a frantic attempt to catch it.

Fetch

Cats love the sound of crumpled paper and playing chase, so this game was made for them. Crumple a piece of paper into a ball and then roll it against the floor, near enough your cat to get his attention. He should be after it like a shot. Vary the distances and speed at which you roll the paper ball to keep your cat interested.

KITTENHOOD AND ADOLESCENCE

" Never pick up a stray kitten . . . unless you've already made up your mind to be owned by it."
—Robert A. Heinlein, writer

*I*n a perfect world, kittens would stay with their mother and littermates for the first eight to 12 weeks of their life. This period helps teach social cues and body language, as well as appropriate limits in play. Rough play is checked by maternal and sibling corrections that teach kittens early on how to interact. A kitten who is separated too early from his mother can make a wonderful pet, but he is typically a needy and dependent cat who may exhibit certain suckling behaviors like kneading, and wool and earlobe sucking (see Chapter 13). He may also nip and bite because he did not have enough time in the nest to learn not to, although this is trainable behavior. Physical development is usually complete around the eight- to ten-month mark, but although your kitten may be at his adult size he may not reach adolescence until approximately 18 months.

Kittens come into this world helpless. During the first weeks of their life, their mother is never far away, and she spends the majority of her time caring for her young. As the kittens begin literally and figuratively to stand on their own feet, their mother continues to teach them. They learn through observation—by mimicking her grooming habits—and by exposure—to their littermates and mother and to the people, animals, and experiences they are socialized to. When your kitten joins your family, you become the main caregiver, responsible for continuing your kitten's education. Start out as you mean to go on, keeping in mind the rules of childraising, also applicable to raising healthy, happy cats: be fair, firm, calm, and consistent.

🐾 Cat Fact

Birth to eight weeks of age is a critical period in a cat's life, with their mother their biggest influence. Remaining with their litter and mother during this period helps give kittens the start they need to become valued feline companions.

BEHIND THE SIGNS

Spaying and Neutering

Before your kitten is seven months is the best time for spaying or neutering. This helps keep your cat safe, as the hormonal changes during adolescence can lead to fighting between neighborhood male cats. It would be very difficult to keep an unneutered male cat indoors if there is an unspayed female in heat nearby, and he is also more likely to display destructive scent-marking behavior in the home. Spaying or neutering also helps lessen the likelihood of our already overcrowded animal shelters being further overburdened unnecessarily.

KITTEN DEVELOPMENT CHART

Birth to Two Weeks, Neonatal Stage:

- Kittens cannot fully see or hear at birth. Their eyes are shut tight, opening gradually during this stage. Their response to sound is minimal at first.
- Newborns are very vulnerable and dependent on their mothers. They have little body strength and sleep most of the time. They cannot eliminate without help from their mother.

Two to Four Weeks, Socialization Stage:

- The mother continues to lick the kittens to stimulate elimination and to groom them.
- The kittens are still weak, but may make exploratory, and wobbly, attempts at movement, generally staying near the warmth of their mother and littermates. The kitten's eyes are open but his vision is not fully developed and his world continues to appears fuzzy and out of focus.
- Starting in this period, kittens should be gently handled daily and slowly introduced to new experiences. Socialization help cats feel comfortable in their world.

Three to Four Weeks, Socialization Stage:

- Walking is introduced around week three but only in the most basic and infrequent way, with kittens still dragging themselves about on their bellies when they do venture away from their mother and littermates.
- In week three their sense of smell is well developed.
- At about four weeks old kittens are able to hold their tails and ears erect. Kittens have improved paw control at this stage; this facilitates "kneading" at their mother to stimulate milk flow.
- Vision is clearer in week four just as the kitten's ability to stand on all four legs has also improved, leading them to explore what is nearby and to play with their littermates.

KITTEN DEVELOPMENT CHART

Five to Seven Weeks, Socialization Stage:	• Kittens are very mobile by week five and very playful. Their mother has less need to stimulate them and she has generally started the process of weaning them. • At about week five, kittens take over their own grooming and may also groom their littermates. • By week six, the kitten's senses are fully developed and the kitten is very responsive to his environment and greatly engaged in play activities. • Kittens are generally weaned from their mother at seven weeks of age, and have transitioned to solid food.
Eight to 12 Weeks: Active Play Period	• Motor coordination is well developed and interaction with littermates continues to play a large part in their development until around week 14. Kittens hone skills through play, such as the ability to hold, mouth, paw, scoop, and toss objects, and to jump and pounce. • Observation skills are put to use, with kittens learning by watching their mother. • Between eight to twelve weeks many kittens leave the nest, moving to new homes.
Three to Six Months, Ranking Stage:	• Kittens start to recognize dominant and submissive ranking within the people and other animals of the household, and may exhibit marking behavior. • Between four and five months of age is often described as the feline equivalent of the "terrible twos" stage that many children go through.
Six to 18 Months, Adolescence:	• Cats begin to leave behind the exuberance of kittenhood during this time. • Kittens are often more aggressive during this period. If not spayed or neutered, sexual behavior begins.

Letting kittens get away with bad behavior only breeds more of the same. It does them no favors. They depend on you to care for them, and that means teaching them appropriate behavior from the start. Keep in mind that kittens don't respond to punishment. They won't associate the punishment with their actions and the only result will be that they learn to mistrust you and their behavior may worsen due to anxiety. Instead, say "no" loudly when your kitten does something inappropriate and withdraw your affection for a short time. That's a message, when delivered consistently, your kitten can understand. Happy and confident adult cats don't just happen. They are a combination of genetics and, more importantly, proper feline parenting by their people.

🐾 Cat Fact

Love and attention are important, but are no substitute for being a good feline parent. Kittens that grow into happy and healthy adults have been socialized, and taught the behavior expected of them.

BEHIND THE SIGNS

Extended Kittenhood

Adolescence occurs between months six and 18, although domesticated cats may continue to exhibit kitten behavior beyond this time. Our felines do not have to hunt for their food and they are generally spayed or neutered, which means they typically live an extended kittenhood and can take their time growing up, unlike cats in the wild.

THE TEENAGE YEARS

During adolescence, hormones contribute to the changed behavior of your cat. Your female cat may become overly affectionate and more vocal when she experiences her first heat cycle, signifying sexual maturity. Your male cat may start spraying indoors—standing up and spraying strong-smelling urine onto vertical surfaces like drapes, walls, and doors, in order to mark his territory. If you are not planning to breed your cat, responsible cat owners will have their cat spayed or neutered before seven months, which also prevents hormone-related behavior like heat cycles and scent marking.

Give your cat plenty of opportunities to play, with and without you, during this time. It can help prevent the problem behavior that may appear at this stage and provides an outlet for his predatory drive. Your cat will experiment during this time to check boundaries. If he plays rough or nips at you, say "no" in a loud voice and then ignore him. Never use physical punishment. You must be consistent in order to teach appropriate behavior and, though it can be hard at first given how cute your cat is, stay strong. Your cat still has some growing up to do and he needs your help to develop into a well-adjusted adult. Watch for the signs of problem behavior and don't make excuses but instead stop problems from the start. Teaching your cat appropriate behavior makes for a better relationship, and an increased bond.

AGES AND STAGES

THE OLDER CAT

"In a cat's eye, all things belong to cats."
—English proverb

As cats enter their senior years, their sleeping patterns may change, they may be less active and interested in what is going on around them, and their temperament may appear changed. The timing for this varies from cat to cat. It is influenced by genetics but—more importantly—by the health of the cat throughout his life. Cats can live to 15-plus years and the signs of age, such as decreased mobility, may be noted in one cat that is ten years of age, while another of the same age is still busily leaping and climbing.

Most cats move as gracefully into old age as they have always lived, although they may now move a little more slowly. His paws and legs may not be as sure-footed as they once were, his coat and muzzle may show signs of gray hair, and he may be slower to respond to sights and sounds. He may appear thinner as he ages, which translates to older cats reacting more sensitively to temperature and hard surfaces.

SIGNS OF AGE

Your aging cat may suffer from arthritis, which results in decreased mobility and may make it difficult for him to get up and down stairs or to his litter box on time. He may exhibit aggressive behavior, even if he has lived his life as a gentle cat. If this is the case, your cat's aggression is typically a sign of age-related pain. He is acting out because of injury and illness, to keep people away. He may recoil from handling and even hide. This behavior is common in older cats but is often treatable, and your veterinarian can provide advice on how to make your senior cat more comfortable. This may include medication, it may involve a few more blankets for his bed, and it may include increased exercise depending on the diagnosis. Cats of any age are creatures of habit, and this is even more true of the older cat, who may have trouble dealing with any change age brings, and act out aggressively as a result.

Sleeping Patterns

Your cat will have slept much of his life away, as cats do, but you may now find that your feline is sleeping more, or less. The latter scenario may be due to pain that is keeping him up, as well as the frequent need to urinate that often accompanies old age and may be preventing him from settling into sleep.

ARTHRITIS: Your cat may be less mobile, particularly in cold and damp weather. His joints may swell, he may limp, and he may avoid being touched. Weight management and exercise can help relieve pain and discomfort, as can having a soft, warm place to sleep and rest. Your veterinarian may also prescribe medication to ease the symptoms, depending on their severity.

CHRONIC RENAL FAILURE: Many older cats experience CRF, which is a deterioration of the kidney function. Your cat may drink more than is normal and urinate more often, and he may lose weight. Treatment includes veterinary assisted/recommended rehydration, diet, and medication.

DENTAL DISEASE: Very common in older cats, this can also be very painful, leading to infection that can be carried from your cat's mouth to his organs. Your cat's appetite may decrease due to mouth pain, which can result in further health issues. Prevention is the best defense and is achieved by keeping your cat's teeth and gums healthy. If he is already suffering swollen gums, pawing at his mouth, or drooling then your veterinarian may recommend removal of any infected teeth to relieve pain. Brush your cat's teeth daily and take him for regular dental exams, to prevent the condition from worsening.

🐾 Cat Fact

Thoughtful owners can counteract age-related problems with attentive care and veterinarian advice.

DIABETES: Your cat may be drinking more than usual, while his appetite is less than it was. He may be losing weight, appear weak, or have bouts of vomiting. If diagnosed, your veterinarian will likely recommend weight management as well as insulin shots or oral medications to manage your cat's insulin levels.

HYPERTHYROIDISM: A common age-related disease, caused by increased production of thyroid hormones. Your cat may appear hyperactive, he may lose weight, vomit, and his appetite will change: he will eat more or less than normal, and his water consumption will increase. Your veterinarian will most often prescribe medication, but may sometimes recommend thyroid surgery.

SENILITY: Just as aging humans suffer from this so too can our cats. Speak to your veterinarian about medication that may help, including homeopathic remedies. This condition is often accompanied by anxiety, for which Rescue Remedy has been proven helpful in some cases. Symptoms include confusion, lack of recognition of his surroundings or people, and aimlessness. Treat your cat with gentle attention when he experiences these episodes and, if you can, distract him with a game. He may not be interested, but if he is it can ease his anxiety.

Your cat's highly developed senses, which he could so long depend on to make him aware of what was going on around him and keep him out of trouble, may be deteriorating and that can be understandably frightening. Although the myth of a cat having nine lives is just that—a myth—his senses will have helped him escape difficult situations throughout his life and he may now be feeling vulnerable, and may act out in aggression as a defensive measure. He may hiss and nip at what he can't see or hear properly, in case it is a threat, and in these cases anti-anxiety medication may help your cat live more comfortably. Some cats adapt easily to deteriorating senses while others may be more fearfully aggressive, but in either case cats will rely more on their remaining senses, such as smell, if their hearing and vision are not as they were. Smell can help cats navigate around quite well, particularly as they are likely moving less and staying close to their bed and

Older Cat Navigation

If your cat is losing his sight he will rely on scent and memory to get around, so this is not the time to make changes in your home. Keep furnishings as they were, and make sure food bowls and his litter box are placed where they always were with no obstacles nearby.

food bowls. Cats that have previously had access to the outdoors should be kept inside for their own safety if their ability to hear is fading, or only be in the yard when supervised by you and on a leash.

This applies to cats that are losing their sight as well, as evidenced if your cat is suddenly bumping into things or is easily startled, although in both these cases— that of the cat with deteriorating hearing or sight—they are unlikely to want to spend much time outside anyway, preferring to stay close. As your cat ages, his world may seem smaller. He will not move around as much and may not observe as much, so spend additional time with him. Help him groom himself, as he may

be having trouble and pet and play with him, using noisy toys if his sight is fading. Older cats can enjoy quality of life and deserve to; they may just need additional help from their people family to do so.

Cat Fact

Most cats may experience fading sight or hearing, but typically do not lose both senses.

GLOSSARY

Breed: A cat classification based on heritage. For example: Siamese or Maine Coon.

Calico: A cat coat with patches of black, red, and white, usually a female cat.

Castrate (neutering): Removal of the male cat's testes.

Cat fancy: The group of people, associations, registries, and clubs involved in showing and breeding cats.

Cobby: A broad, round body type with a broad head and shorter legs. For example, the Persian.

Colorpoint: A coat pattern where the face mask, ears, tail, and feet are darker in color than the lighter color on the body.

Crossbreed, crossbreeding, crossbred: Refers to a cat whose parents are from two different breeds or (crossbreeding) the mating of cats of two different breeds or varieties, such as random-bred cats with pedigreed breeds, or domestic cats with wild cats. Offspring from this breeding are known as hybrids.

Dam (queen): Mother of a litter.

Dander: Small skin scales that can cause an allergic reaction in sensitive individuals.

Defensive-aggressive: Fear-based aggressive behavior that is directed at any perceived challenge.

Domestic: An animal that has become adapted to humans over many generations. May also refer to a cat without pedigree.

Dominance: Assertive and superiority behavior directed at people and animals.

Dominant-aggressive: Overconfident and threatening aggressive behavior that is directed at any perceived challenge.

Double coat: A coat with a thick layer of awn and down hairs (undercoat) underneath the top guard hairs (overcoat).

Down: A secondary hair type that is very soft, slightly wavy, and is usually much shorter than the top guard hairs and mats much more easily.

Ear Carriage: The way the cat's ears are held: erect, back, flattened. Can indicate mood and intentions combined with other body language cues.

Ear Mange: Condition caused by ear mites, causes itching and scratching. Ear appearance is red and can be crusty.

Ear Mites: A tiny parasite that is attracted to the ear canal of cats, and causes intense itching and irritation.

Felidae: The cat family.

Felis: A genus of the family Felidae.

***Felis silvestris catus*:** The scientific name given to the domestic cat.

Feral: A cat born in the wild or who reverted to a wild state.

Guard hairs: They form the coat's protective outer layer and are the longest of the three hair types.

Heat: A queen's estrus period, when she is receptive to the advances of an unneutered male cat.

Hot Spots: Surface skin infections common to

cats; they generally appear as circular patches and can be painfully itchy.

Hybrid: A cross between two different breeds. Can refer to the offspring that result from the breeding of two different breeds or two different species.

Inbred: Cats who have been mated to very close relatives.

Intact: Unneutered, unaltered.

Litter: A group of kittens born together to the same queen. May also refer to the material used in cat litter boxes.

Mackerel tabby: A tabby pattern with narrow parallel stripes that run down the cat's sides.

Moggy (moggie): Mixed-breed, cross-bred, or random-bred cat. Not a pedigreed cat.

Muzzle: The nose and jaw.

Neuter: To surgically render sterile.

Outcrossing: Mating a pedigree cat of one breed to a cat of a different breed in order to strengthen the breed or introduce new traits.

Paw pads: The furless padded areas on the bottom of the cat's feet. Cats sweat through their paw pads.

Pedigree: The official written record of a cat's ancestry.

Purebred: A cat with parents of the same breed.

Queen: An unspayed female cat.

Scent Marking: Use of urine and sweat to mark territory, and communicate with other cats.

Separation Anxiety: Fear or anxiety-based condition in which cats exhibit distress and behavior problems when left alone.

Single Coat: Coat that is one layer thick, with no undercoat.

Single-coated: A cat that has little or no undercoat, for example, the Balinese.

Socialization: The exposure of cats to new people, animals, and places, to aid in their healthy development.

Spay: To neuter a female cat.

Spraying: Using urine to mark territory, usually onto a vertical surface. Both male and female cats may spray, although the behavior is more common in males that have not been neutered.

Tipped: A coat type in which the hairs have colored ends.

Triple-coated: A coat type in which the awn, down, and guard hairs are all the same length, for example, the coat of the Siberian.

Undercoat: A dense second coat that is underneath the topcoat.

Wild: Often used to describe a feral cat. A wild cat is not domesticated.

ACKNOWLEDGMENTS

hank you to family and friends: Maryann, Glenn, Jen, Quinn, Jack, Beth, Gord, Chrysi, Clifford, Bowen, Lindsey, Ben, Joanne, Lorraine. And thank you to Ali, Richard, and James at Quid.

PICTURE CREDITS

Cover	© Ali Walper	43 Left	© Marilyna | Dreamstime
8	© Kati1313 | Dreamstime	44	© Levin | Dreamstime
9	© Reticent | Dreamstime	45	© Vlue | Dreamstime
10	© Marilyna | Dreamstime	46	© Neotakezo | Dreamstime
11 Left	© Wrangel | Dreamstime	47	© Unteroffizier | Dreamstime
11 Right	© Barmaley111 | Dreamstime	48	© Focalexus | Dreamstime
13 Left	© Tatyanagl | Dreamstime	49 Left	© Isselee | Dreamstime
13 Right	© Kipuxa | Dreamstime	49 Right	© Linqong | Dreamstime
14 Right	© Pepperbox | Dreamstime (and throughout)	50	© Sbotas | Dreamstime
		51	© Inspire9000 | Dreamstime
15	© Mayangsari | Dreamstime	52	© Argument | Dreamstime
16	© Ldambles | Dreamstime	54	© Nndemidchick | Dreamstime
17 Left	© Denisnata | Dreamstime	55	© Linncurrie | Dreamstime
18	© Emprise | Dreamstime	56	© Bedo | Dreamstime
21 Top-left	© Isselee | Dreamstime	57	© Gravicapa | Dreamstime
22 Top-right	© Flibustier | Dreamstime	59	© Miraswonderland | Dreamstime
22 Bottom-left	© Scantynebula | Dreamstime		
22 Bottom-right	© Isselee | Dreamstime	60	© Lihital | Dreamstime
23 Top-left	© Eriklam | Dreamstime	61 Left	© Kipuxa | Dreamstime
23 Bottom	© Kirza | Dreamstime	62	© Noonie | Dreamstime
24 Top-left	© Isselee | Dreamstime	63	© Ioooloo | Dreamstime
24 Top-right	© Krissilundgren | Dreamstime	64	© Inspirator88 | Dreamstime
24 Bottom-left	© Isselee | Dreamstime	65 Right	© Allkindza | iStockphoto
24 Bottom-right	© Katarinache | Dreamstime	66	© Kertis | Dreamstime
25 Left	© Kovalvs | Dreamstime	67	© Lisapics | iStockphoto
25 Right	© Linncurrie | Dreamstime	68	© Qbanczyk | iStockphoto
26 Left	© Emprise | Dreamstime	69	© Ankimo | Dreamstime
26 Top-right	© Sazonov | Dreamstime	71	© Fallenangel | Dreamstime
26 Bottom-right	© Isselee | Dreamstime	72	© Eriklam | Dreamstime
28	© Linncurrie | Dreamstime	73	© Marilyna | Dreamstime
29 Right	© Alexsaberi | Dreamstime	74	© Suerob | Dreamstime
30	© Scantynebula | iStockphoto	75 Left	© Selestte | Dreamstime
32	© Linqong | Dreamstime	75	© Jane Burton | NaturePL
34	© Blueee | Dreamstime	76	© Selestte | Dreamstime
35	© Magdanatka | Dreamstime	77	© Adamedwards | Dreamstime
37	© Ksoloits | Dreamstime		
38	© Skynesher | iStockphoto	78	© Actionsport | Dreamstime
39	© Littlemacproductions | Dreamstime	79	© C-foto | Dreamstime
		80 Left	© Spat78 | Dreamstime
41	© VMJones | iStockphoto	81	© Dreamframer | Dreamstime
42	© Yurchyk | Dreamstime		

BIBLIOGRAPHY

Alger, Janet, and Steven Alger, *Cat Culture.* Philadelphia: Temple University Press, 2003.

Bailey, Gwen, *What Is My Cat Thinking.* California: Thunder Bay Press, 2002.

Becker, Marty, and Gina Spadafori, *Why Do Cats Always Land On Their Feet.* Florida: Health Communications, Inc., 2006.

Bonham, Margaret, *The Cat Owner's Problem Solver.* New Jersey: T.F.H. Publications, 2008.

Budiansky, Stephen, *The Character Of Cats.* New York: Penguin Group, 2002.

Case, Linda, *The Cat.* Iowa: Iowa State Press, 2003.

Christensen, Wendy, *Outwitting Cats.* Connecticut: Globe Pequot Press, 2004.

Dodman, Nicholas, *The Cat Who Cried For Help.* New York: Bantam Books, 1999.

Edgar, Jim, *Bad Cat.* New York: Workman Publishing Company, 2004.

Helgren, J. Anne, *Communicating With Your Cat.* New York: Barron's Educational Series, 1999.

Hotchner, Tracie, *The Cat Bible.* New York: Gotham Books, 2007.

Houpt, Katherine, *Domestic Animals Behavior for Veterinarians and Animal Scientists.* Iowa: Iowa State University Press, 1991.

Johnson-Bennett, Pam, *Cat Vs. Cat.* New York: Penguin Group, 2004.

Johnson-Bennett, Pam, *Starting From Scratch.* New York: Penguin Group, 2007.

Johnson-Bennett, Pam, *Think Like A Cat.* New York: Penguin Group, 2000.

Johnson-Bennett, Pam, *Twisted Whisker.* California: The Crossing Press, 1999.

Kalstone, Shirlee, and John Martin, *Good Cat!* New Jersey: Wiley Publishing Inc., 2005.

Lachman, Larry, *Cats On The Counter.* New York: St. Martin's Press, 2000.

Moore, Arden, *The Cat Behavior Answer Book.* Massachusetts: Storey Publishing, 2007.

Morris, Desmond, *Catwatching.* New York: Three Rivers Press, 1986

Rainbolt, Dusty, *Cat Wrangling Made Easy.*
Connecticut: Globe Pequot Press, 2008.

Samson, Gary, and Dick Wolfsie, *Cat
Conundrums.* Cincinnati: Emmis Books, 2005.

Tabor, Roger, *Understanding Cat Behavior.*
Ohio: David & Charles, 2003.

Turner, Dennis, and Patrick Bateson,
The Domestic Cat. New York:
Cambridge University Press, 2000.

ARTICLES: PRINT AND WEB

Driscoll, Carlos, David Macdonald, and Stephen
O'Brien, "From Wild Animals To Domestic Pets,
An Evolutionary View Of Domestication." *Proc
Natl Acad Sci*, v.106, no.1, 9971–9978, 2009.

Moelk, Mildred, "Vocalizing in the House-
Cat; A Phonetic and Functional Study."
The American Journal of Psychology,
vol. 57, no.2,184–205,1944.

"Cat Owners More Educated Than Dog
Owners," www.telegraph.co.uk/science/
science-news/7165164/Cat-owners-more-
educated-than-dog-owners.html. *Telegraph
Science*. Retrieved July 23, 2010.

"Oldest Known Pet Cat? 9500-Year-
Old Burial Found on Cyprus," http://
news.nationalgeographic.com/
news/2004/04/0408_040408_oldestpetcat.
html. *National Geographic News*.
Retrieved July 20, 2010.

"What Does Your Cat Really Do
While You're Away?"
www.nydailynews.com/lifestyle/pets/2009/
12/04/2009-12-04_what_does_your_cat_
really_do_while youre_away_not_many_
catnaps_kitty_cam_study_f.html. *NY Daily
News Lifestyle*, Retrieved June 25, 2010.

"Why Do Cats Purr?" www.scientificamerican.
com/article.cfm?id=why-do-cats-purr.
Scientific American, Retrieved July 12, 2010.

"Cats," www.humanesociety.org/animals/
cats. *Humane Society of the United
States*, Retrieved July 6, 2010.

"Cat Care," www.aspca.org/pet-care/cat-care.
*The American Society for the Prevention of
Cruelty to Animals*, Retrieved July 4, 2010.

"People," www.cia.gov/library/publications/the-
world-factbook/geos/uk.html. Central Intelligence
Agency World Factbook, Retrieved July 12, 2010.

INDEX